NAVIGATING
in organizations:

How to impact organizations and get things done!

Trent Press

Navigating in Organizations:
How to Impact Organizations and Get Things Done!
All Rights Reserved.
Copyright © 2016 Gary T. Moore
v4.0

Cover Photo © 2016 thinkstockphotos.com. All rights reserved - used with permission.
Interior graphic images by FreePik (www. freepik.com). Used with permission per their Terms of Use. Altered/customized by Marilyn Anderson.

ISBN: 978-0-578-17304-7

PRINTED IN THE UNITED STATES OF AMERICA

To the reader…

No wait, let me rephrase that.

To the person who is trying to decide whether to read this book. The principles and tactics in this book are targeted to help you if you:

- Have joined a company, a club, a committee, a nonprofit organization, a school or university (as faculty, administrator, or student), a board of directors, or another type of organization…and you want to help "make positive things happen."
- Want to be a leader in whatever organization you're involved with.
- Are already a leader, but want to be more effective.
- Just began (or are about to begin) a new job or career, and want a "head start."
- Have found yourself saying, "Why don't they listen to my ideas?"
- Are frustrated with "organizational politics."
- Are tired of attending mind-numbing, pointless meetings.
- See your organization struggling and want to help turn things around.
- Are fed up with the slow pace of change in your organization.
- Simply want to make a positive impact (i.e. get things done!) on an organization.

This is a hands-on book based on my fifty years of experience making a positive impact and assuming leadership positions in every organization I've joined. That includes two major corporations; one medium-sized business in which I had leadership roles for twenty years, purchased, ran profitably for over nine more years, and then successfully sold; the boards of directors of one national trade association (where I served as board president), one local trade association, four nonprofit organizations (I served as board president of three), three churches, one fraternity, two clubs (I served as president of one), and countless committees (including creating and chairing two successful, major fund-raisers for nonprofit organizations serving children).

Through this experience, I've learned how to get things done in organizations, how to assume leadership roles, and then how to help the organizations achieve their objectives.

With this book, you'll have a head start on making a positive impact on whatever organization you're a part of—or that you want to be a part of.

Gary T. Moore
December 2015

# INTRODUCTION

Most of the world's work is done through organizations, including companies, clubs, boards of directors, nonprofits, religious organizations, trade associations, sports teams and leagues, volunteer groups,political parties, governing bodies, agencies and departments, homeowners associations, PTAs, the military, committees, departments, co-ops, fraternities, sororities, informal organizations without names – the list is endless.

You may join organizations for a variety of reasons, including to advance your personal objectives or agenda; help the organization meet its objectives; socialize; network; advance your career; have fun; add structure to your life; earn income; express religious beliefs; make the world a better place; or a myriad of other reasons. Regardless of which organization you're involved with, and whatever the reason you joined, you need to ask yourself three key questions:

- *How can I be more effective within that organization, make a positive impact, and meet my objectives while helping the organization meet its objectives?*
- *What skills should I develop in order to make that positive impact?*
- *What things should I avoid doing?*

Throughout this book, I'll give you real-world answers to these pressing questions and help you formulate customized actions that fit with your individual situation.

Every organization is unique and comes complete with its own characteristics, idiosyncrasies, and specific operations. Some organizations are well developed and sophisticated, while others are less so. Some organizations are short lived, perhaps days or weeks in duration, while others last decades or longer. The members of some organizations can fit into one conference room, while others have members spread out across the nation or globe. Some organizations lack formal structure, while others, such as the military, have extremely rigid structures. The principles and practices outlined here must be adapted to your specific situation. However, organizations have enough common characteristics to make the principles and practices in this book an important reference as you work and participate in the organizations you choose to join.

Organizations are...

By definition, most organizations are <u>structured</u> and <u>hierarchical</u> in nature. There is "pecking order" within each of them. However, don't be deceived by the organization chart. No matter how carefully or creatively drawn, a chart is only a superficial description of the organization's hierarchy. And even organizations that don't seem to have structure or hierarchy (or an organization chart) do have structure and hierarchy. People within organizations gain formal or informal status and power due to a variety of things, including: designation by a governing body such as a board of directors; position or title; knowledge; access to people and information; experience; age; personality; "time in place"; relationships; assertiveness; willingness to put in the time, do hard things, take risks; ability to persuade and sell ideas; enthusiasm; work ethic, and so forth.

One of the first steps to take as a new entrant at any organization involves a simple glance at the organization chart (if there is one). From there, observe as the organization's *real* hierarchy plays out daily. This is sometimes called the "informal organization." In George Orwell's novel *Animal Farm* (originally copyrighted 1945), the farmyard animals overthrew the farmer hierarchy in favor of a utopian, all-animal, non-hierarchical world. Orwell then described the new...you guessed it...hierarchy as "All animals are equal, but some animals are more equal than others." In his book the "pigs" were the "more equal" animals…and even within the pig herd there was a hierarchy. It's good to learn who is "more equal" in any organization you are part of or interface with.

Learning the hierarchy is important because organizations are <u>political</u>. It's not uncommon to hear "I hate the politics in that organization" or, "I hate office politics." Get over it. Any group made up of individuals has politics. Politics is the formal and informal way alliances are built, compromises are structured, decisions are made. Yes, there can be toxic politics, where everything meaningful is handled behind closed doors; or where paths and plans are blocked by the informal organization. However, in most organizations the politics are relatively open and, when practiced by skilled practitioners, useful in getting things done. You want to be one of those skilled practitioners.

Organizations are <u>social</u> in nature. After all, they are comprised of people. In general, people are more effective in organizations when they are working with people they like and respect. That doesn't mean everyone (or anyone for that matter) in an organization must, can, or should be your friend; that's impractical and undesirable. However, to be effective you will need to acknowledge the social aspect of the organization and pick your spots to plug into the social network…both the personal network and the digital network.

Organizations are <u>competitive.</u> Competitiveness is a natural human trait. Watch a group of schoolchildren naturally determine who runs faster, answers more questions, or has more "stuff." While competition can be destructive if it runs rampant and if it is only self-serving, it can also be an element in organizations that spurs individuals and organizations to progress.

In the sense used here, the word "competitive" does not necessarily mean competing to determine winners and losers. It does mean that individuals in organizations compete for resources: they compete to get noticed, to gain recognition, to advance their agendas, to contribute, and to win leadership positions. Healthy competition can bring out extra effort, new ideas, and the best in people – all with the goal of moving the organization forward. The key is to compete *without* damaging the organization or the personal, professional relationships that are so critical both to your – and the organization's – effectiveness.

Organizations are not...

In popular culture or literature, there are misconceptions about organizations that can set up unrealistic expectations. This brief discussion is to explain what organizations are <u>not</u>, to help avoid these misconceptions.

Organizations are <u>not families</u>.

It is often said about some organizations – particularly smaller businesses and nonprofit organizations – that "we're all family," "we're just family," or

"we treat everyone like family."

These statements are probably not true (unless, of course, all the organization's members really are legally family!). Why? Because family is a whole different dynamic. Healthy families imply unconditional love. Families often accept every member, warts and all. Unhealthy families can engender resentment and hatred. Generally, none of these emotions – unconditional love, resentment, hatred, acceptance, "warts and all" – are characteristics of effective organizations.

In effective organizations, if you're not perceived as meeting expectations, you can be quickly asked to leave. In effective organizations, leaders and others are making judgments about your performance from the minute you come in contact with the organization, and even before you are part of the organization. In most families, performance is not the criteria for membership or acceptance.

Organizations are <u>not meritocracies</u> (i.e., the holding of power, position, or status by people selected strictly on the basis of their ability).

In even the most effective organizations, "Let the best man (or woman) win" is not a routine outcome. There are too many political, social, and relationship variables that come into play here. And, whether discussing individuals, plans of action, or ideas, there are many perceptions of what "best" really is. While an organization's guiding principles should include acknowledging and promoting the "best" based on merit, this doesn't always happen. In fact, since effective organizations require individuals with different and interlocking skill sets, an organization of "bests" is not always effective. Teams where everyone is an "all-star" can be fun, but they're not usually the ones that win championships.

To be effective in organizations you have to be good (maybe even the best) at what you do. But you also have to be good at organizational practices and skills, and avoid taking counterproductive actions. That's what this book is all about.

Relationships, relationships, relationships

As you read this book, you will find that one theme persists across all chapters: Effective organizations, positive impact by individuals within organizations, and productive transactions between organizations are all built on individual relationships. Put simply:

> *People work most effectively with people they*
> *know, like, believe, understand, and trust.*

In sports, this may be called teamwork or "a good locker room."

In corporations it may be called "culture."

In relationships between individuals, it may be called "chemistry."

I like to use the term *personal, professional relationships*. These are bonds that are professional, but that have an interpersonal "touch." The importance of *personal, professional relationships* is evidenced at the highest levels. In contemporary politics, there is endless discussion about personal and professional relationships (or, a lack of them) between the President and members of Congress; between the President and leaders of other countries; between stars on sports teams; and between leaders of all types of interfacing organizations.

It's important to note that healthy personal, professional relationships are not necessarily built on spending a lot of personal time together. Consider this real-life example:

> I worked for twenty years for two very different brothers. One was a champion swimmer and the other rode motorcycles across multiple continents. One was more outgoing and the other was more reserved. I didn't have much in common with either brother on a personal interest level. I'm a hiker, a reader, and a golfer. We spent little personal time together. However, we built personal, professional relationships based on acknowledgment of our individual strengths and weaknesses, and based on trust. We were interested in each other personally ... but at a professional, respectful "distance." These relationships helped drive our company to national leadership and excellence in our industry.

No matter what the organization, healthy personal, professional relationships between people in key positions make the organizational machinery work effectively. Unhealthy or nonexistent personal, professional relationships can destroy organizational effectiveness. You can begin making these relationships on the day you join an organization, and at whatever level you join.

The first chapter in the How-to section of this book focuses on building personal, professional relationships. And while the old real estate cliché is that the three most important things are "location, location, location," the three most critical components of effective organizations are "relationships, relationships, relationships."

How to use this book

This book has three main sections:

- **How-to** section with chapters for each of ten identified best practices for effectively navigating in organizations and making a positive impact.
- **Don't** section with chapters for eleven common but counterproductive practices that make individuals ineffective in organizations and contribute to overall organizational ineffectiveness.
- **Skills** section that identifies nine skills to develop in order to effectively navigate in organizations.

I've added a **Bonus** section on how to build a **personal board of advisors.**

Most chapters begin with an **Overview** of key points on that topic; followed by **The Details**, with more specifics; and **Real-World Experiences** (i.e., summaries of real-life examples of the principles in that chapter). While the names (except where I am personally referenced) and some details have been changed, these Real-World Experiences really happened. Where it makes sense, many chapters end with **Get Started** suggested actions to get you moving on that concept, and a list of **Resources** for more detailed study on that chapter's topic.

You can use this book any way that you want to, but I'd suggest first reviewing the Overview portions of each chapter. Then, dig into The Details and Real-World Experiences that seem most immediately relevant; check out the Resources listed, and take action on the Get Started items. Keep this book handy as your experiences in organizations resonate with sections of this book.

Let's get to work!
Let's get "organized!"

TABLE OF CONTENTS

How to......

Organizational "Don't's"

Don't:

Skills to Effectively Navigate in Organizations

H♥W TO...
instructions for navigating

HOW TO BUILD PERSONAL, PROFESSIONAL RELATIONSHIPS

The Overview

All organizations function on the basis of relationships among their members, and between their members and individuals outside the organization, to thrive and grow. Quite simply, people interface most effectively, and prefer to interface consistently with, people they *know, like, believe, understand, and trust.*

Friendship is not the goal of developing personal, professional organizational relationships. Friendship is too rare and not usually planned. However, you can strive to develop strong, working relationships with others in your organization. These often begin by developing rapport. And part of building rapport with others is developing empathy. If you were in their place, what would you be interested in? What would your concerns be? What would your perspective be?

What's the payoff for taking the time to form these relationships? It comes in many forms, including:

- Exchange of ideas
- Synergy from people with different perspectives, skills, backgrounds, and ideas working together toward common goals
- Sounding boards for your ideas and points of view
- Mutual support for ideas or initiatives
- Networking

- Honest feedback
- Mentoring
- "Heads-up" information about things happening in the organization... and elsewhere
- Insights into the organization that can't be obtained otherwise
- Loyalty
- Conflict reduction within the organization
- Easier management of conflicts when they do arise
- Personal satisfaction

The Details

When you join an organization, you should take the initiative to reach out to others in that organization to begin forming personal, professional relationships. Conversely, you should also be open to the overtures of others who reach out to you. Once initiated, relationships need to be "intentionalized" (I made that word up) over time.

Building and maintaining personal, professional relationships is so critical to your success and that of your organization that you should **assume 100 percent of the responsibility for forming and maintaining the personal, professional relationships you find important, useful, and appropriate.** This chapter summarizes thirteen tips for doing just that. Though specific practices such as these can be helpful and effective tools, the basic principle is to *focus on the other person,* not yourself. It's all about others – not all about you!

Tip #1

Remember the basic rules for establishing good initial rapport with anyone:

- Give a strong handshake and use eye contact when meeting someone in person.

- Dress appropriately for the situation and group. How do you want to present yourself? How would others expect you to dress for this group and situation?

- Use professional etiquette when contacting by phone. Ask if it's a good time to talk; leave voice mail messages when not connecting; speak distinctly; give clear return contact information.

- Don't substitute purely electronic communication for appropriate personal communication. Create opportunities to meet others in person, or synchronously over the phone (or via computer communication such as Skype) , at least once if at all possible. Use electronic communication (email, Twitter, Facebook, texting, LinkedIn…) to support and build the relationship.

- Acknowledge and congratulate others' accomplishments, awards, and positive publicity.

- Send personal thank-you/congratulatory notes or electronic communication (handwritten and mailed notes are one way to cut through the electronic "noise" of communication. They get noticed because they are so rare).

Tip #2

Be aware of three personal needs/objective areas of others, and help them meet those needs:

- Organizational (what goals do they have for the organization, and for themselves within the organization?)

- Social (what do they enjoy socially?)

- Ego-centered (if high ego, gently feed it; if you see a need for ego support, then support it)

Tip #3

Ask open-ended questions…about others. Be inquisitive and show honest interest in them.

What interested you in this organization, company, or activity?

What do you do for fun?

What do you do when you're not working with this organization?

Where are you from?

Where did you go to school?

What professional achievements are you proudest of?

What professional goals do you have?

What are your biggest challenges in your work?

Tell me the {insert other person's name} story.

What would you like to know about me?

Tip #4

Find one or more common interests: a book, movie, or gaming genre; a sports team; a leisure time activity; an organizational interest outside of your common organization; background or place of origin; educational institution or major; other mutual contacts. Find something to facilitate conversation and ultimately facilitate building a relationship.

Tip #5

Learn and match their style: Personal first, then professional; or professional first, then personal.

Realize that some people will want to get to know you personally before working with you on significant organizational transactions. Others want to "take care of business first" before connecting on a personal level. Determine which is appropriate for each relationship, and then interact that way.

Tip #6

Match the pace and intensity of others using the following signals:

- Speech patterns
- Communication form and responsiveness
- Communication frequency
- Body language
- Organizational versus personal communication

Tip #7

Find out how individuals like to communicate, and then communicate in that manner. For example, if they prefer text, then text. If they prefer email, use email. If they want to meet in person, schedule an appointment.

Regardless of someone's preferred method of communication, it's important to have some face-to-face time with anyone with whom you want develop a strong, professional relationship. Once you've laid that groundwork, then text, email, phone, or any other method can be used effectively to deepen and maintain the relationship.

Tip #8

Reveal some things about yourself and your own interests, all the while looking for points of connection with others. Here are some conversation starters to consider:

I struggled with time management in school, but eventually developed a system that seems to work.

I'm currently reading…

I'm frustrated by…

I enjoy hiking on weekends.

I miss my family.

I love this organization because…

Tip #9

Keep commitments. Do what you say you're going to do, when you say you're going to do it. If you can't meet a commitment, take the initiative to let the other person or the organization know as soon as you know.

When making time commitments to respond with information, return a call, handle a problem, or some other time-sensitive issue, avoid using the phrases "as soon as possible" or "as soon as I can." These are clichés that mean different things to different people…but don't really mean anything. People sometimes read these statements as meaning "I'll get back to you when it's convenient for me." Instead, use phrases like, "I'll call you back no later than Friday at 2 PM with that information." Get the other person's agreement that this is an appropriate time frame (or, modify as needed). Then, do it.

Tip #10

Seek out and create opportunities for "offline" time together. Coffee, breakfast, or lunch are all good starting points. Sporting events or other activities are good opportunities as relationships progress. Do something the other person wants to do or enjoys, even if you don't.

Tip #11

Find a way to do something for the individuals with whom you are building relationships. Help with a problem. Make a connection or referral for them. Support an interest of theirs.

Be ready to graciously accept and say thank you when someone does something for you. Don't feel you always have to return a favor. Often the best "thank you" is a simple "Thank you." However, over time, the best relationships naturally maintain some proportionate reciprocity of exchanges.

Tip #12

Make connections for others. Introduce them to people who can help them personally or professionally. Go out of your way to do this and you'll find that others will begin to reciprocate the favor.

Tip #13

Use humor – carefully. Humor in relationships is seldom joke-telling. The best humor is often self-deprecation, or gentle kidding about non-sensitive subjects. More about this in the Skills section of this book.

Real-World Experience

<u>*Gary the engineer*</u>

When I joined a sales organization after obtaining my engineering degree, I was laser-focused on doing this job. I gathered information on customer needs and prepared outstanding sales proposals that "proved" my stuff was best. I avoided small talk with customers, thinking this was a waste of time. Likewise, I avoided spending time with more experienced salespeople or supplier representatives (i.e., another waste of time).

Despite my engineering degree, work ethic, and focus, I was not succeeding.

Finally, Leslie, an experienced salesperson with the company, offered to make sales calls with me to observe my style. Working with Leslie, I began to develop a personal, professional relationship as we rode to customers' locations and had lunch or coffee together. We began to "get to know each other" on a level other than strictly business. Over coffee one afternoon, Leslie told me the thing that was standing in my way was not my technical knowledge, my time management, or my focus. It was my unwillingness to form personal, professional relationships with customers, fellow salespeople, and suppliers.

"Gary, it's not about the stuff or the proposals, it's about the relationships. Customers want to trust you before they buy from you. You don't give them a chance to do that. Also, you are cutting yourself off from mentoring by experienced salespeople and supplier representatives because, frankly, they don't know if they like you or not, and they tend to go out of their way to help people whom they like."

I began to slow down, focus on other people instead of just the stuff. I began to form personal, professional relationships. I began to succeed.

Peter and Brenda

Shortly after being elected to the board of directors for her private club, Linda was contacted via email by Peter. He'd been on the board for a couple of years, and even though they had not yet met personally, Peter emailed Linda to invite her to coffee (using electronic communication to reach out and set up a personal interface).

Over coffee, Peter asked Linda why she had been interested in the board, what her other interests were, and what she'd like to accomplish for the club while on the board. Linda asked Peter about his work, his career, and his vision for the club. They developed rapport, and found that they shared an interest in working with nonprofit organizations that benefit young people.

They gave each other referrals for their outside interests, and attended events benefiting each other's nonprofit interests (proportionate reciprocity). They maintained contact between board meetings through email and phone calls. Linda became a supporter of Peter's proposals on the board and helped him structure those through her communication skills. They worked together outside of board meetings to get tasks accomplished at formal board meetings. Their relationship helped move the club forward in a positive direction, and benefitted each other in activities beyond the club.

Following their terms on the board, they maintained contact through email and phone communication, periodically supplemented and supported by lunch or coffee together. Peter mentored Brenda in her fund-raising and leadership activities outside the club. Peter was a great fund-raiser. Brenda continued to use her communication skills to help Peter with his community projects.

<u>Franklin and Winston; Ulysses and William T.</u>

Among organizations at the highest levels, there are clear examples where personal, professional relationships changed history.

Franklin Roosevelt and Winston Churchill began developing a personal, professional relationship before they were part of the same organization, using the communication technology of the time — letters and telegrams. Then they met personally. They built and maintained their relationship over long distances and times, using phone calls, letters, and telegrams, supplemented periodically by direct personal interface. They continued to explore common as well as conflicting views of the world while they led the Allies to victory in WWII. Their personal, professional relationship was crucial to the Allies' victory.

Generals Ulysses S. Grant and William T. Sherman of the Union Army developed a close personal, professional relationship during the Civil War. Grant protected Sherman when he was accused of instability. Sherman defended Grant when he was accused of drunkenness. After the relationship was developed, they were seldom in the same room together during the war. They communicated and supported their relationship electronically via telegrams…the "email" of the time. Together, they commanded the armies that ultimately saved the Union. Mutual respect and trust were key.

Each of these personal, professional relationships…both of which changed the world…did develop into friendships. But only after years of mutual respect and working together.

Resources

How to Win Friends and Influence People
Written by Dale Carnegie and originally published in 1936, with several updates since then, this book remains one of the best how-to books for developing positive relationships with others. It periodically appears on best-seller lists, even today.

Franklin and Winston: An Intimate Portrait of an Epic Friendship
A book written by Jon Meacham, originally published January 4, 2004, copyright 2003.

Get Started

1. Identify three people you would like to explore a personal, professional relationship with in organizations where you are a member.

2. Reach out to schedule coffee or other face-to-face meeting for a personal, professional conversation.

3. Think of a personal or professional connection you can make for each of them.

HOW TO GET POSITIVE ORGANIZATIONAL EXPOSURE… WITHOUT LOOKING LIKE A SELF-PROMOTING JERK

The Overview

Your objectives in an organization may include:

- Advance the organization
- Advance <u>in</u> the organization
- Advance the objectives of the organization

Whatever your objectives, at some point you will be more effective and make more positive contributions if you are noticed – in a good way. On the other hand, you do not want to be noticed as a person who is simply trying to advance himself or herself, or who is feeding their ego, or who is insensitive to the time or interests of others.

A key to getting positive organizational notice without appearing like a self-promoting jerk is to do the things that get positive notice while simultaneously advancing the organization and its objectives. In order for your actions to be good for you and your position in the organization…they must also be good for the organization. Here are some of those actions:

The Details

- **Simply excel at your job or assignment.**

One way to get noticed positively in an organization is to simply and quietly go about doing and excelling at your job or assignment, while avoiding spending lots of organization time on personal issues, social media, or other distractions.

Do your job and do it well.

Duh.

This focus on the work at hand is even more effective when combined with one of the other actions covered in this section!

- **Find a niche where your skills and knowledge can make a difference. Offer to help in that area.**

Everyone brings a unique set of skills, knowledge, and contacts to an organization. Look for an area in the organization where your skills contribute, and then reach out and offer to help in that area. The possibilities include organizational skills, finance, networking contacts, topical or industry-specific knowledge, technical skills, speaking, report writing, sales... Identify what you do well that can make an immediate impact, and then focus on that area.

- **Contribute your tech skills early.**

Most younger people bring technology and social media skills that are well beyond the scope of an organization's older members. When you see a need, offer your tech skills. Maybe you can work on a website, manage a data base, mentor older employees on tech issues, help develop a social media presence, or lend guidance on a technology upgrade project. This can lead to positive attention quickly.

Real-World Experience

<u>*Marketing skills, fresh out of school*</u>

Kim joined a small, family-owned company's customer service department and immediately noticed a scarcity of effective marketing materials. The website was poorly designed and not attracting traffic; there was no social media presence; and the company graphics were dull. Kim had developed marketing skills in college, having set up website and social media presences for several clubs that she participated in. She also knew a good graphic designer. After a few weeks on the job, she initiated a meeting with the sales manager, showed him some of her work, and offered to help the company upgrade in all these areas. After some discussion, the work was assigned to Kim. Her career was officially launched.

- **Take on unpleasant tasks and do them well.**

Most of us have heard the sarcastic phrase: "It's a dark and lonely job, but someone has to do it."

In most organizations, there are indeed "dark and lonely jobs." These are tasks that folks would rather not do because they are difficult, unpleasant, and lack glamour. However, when someone responds positively when asked to handle one of these tasks (or better yet, volunteers or simply assumes the responsibility without complaining), three things usually happen:

- The task gets done.
- The person doing the task gets that learning experience.
- The person doing the task gets noticed – particularly if they report back on results of the task.

When you identify one of these difficult or unpleasant tasks in an organization, consider taking it on. The task will get done. You will get the experience. You will probably be noticed, positively. The organization will be more effective because of it.

Real-World Experience

<u>The Bowling Fund-raiser</u>

I was new on the board of a nonprofit organization that served children. I had volunteered for the Development (fund-raising) Committee, without having much experience in this area. It seemed like important work, and others seemed to avoid it. I thought I might learn something.

Then, the idea surfaced to conduct the first Bowlathon fund-raiser in the area to benefit the nonprofit. I was asked to chair the event. Gulp! I had never managed such an event before. And, I hate bowling. However, after some consideration, I agreed. I called on the experience of others inside and outside the organization to mentor me and help make it happen. It turned out to be a very difficult assignment, consuming more time and effort than I had imagined. It was also a success beyond my and the organization's expectations. From that point forward I was acknowledged as a leader on that board and two years later became president. I was able to lead the organization in the directions I felt were most appropriate. All because I agreed to take on a difficult task and did it well.

<u>The sales manager collects past-due bills</u>

As new sales manager for a growing company, Barry needed information and cooperation from the Finance Department, but he was struggling to connect and get their help.

Then he overheard the head of the Finance Department lamenting about two of his biggest frustrations: collecting past-due bills from customers and getting salespersons' cooperation in the process. Collecting past-due bills was indeed an unpleasant task (a dark and lonely job, if you will).

Barry jumped on the opportunity by volunteering to help collect past-due invoices. He set up a system to ensure sales' future involvement in the process. Barry focused and devoted time to this every day. He brought his people skills to bear on this difficult task. It wasn't sales glamour, but it got the attention of the head of finance and the company CEO.

When salespeople started getting their commission checks faster, they came to appreciate and emulate Barry's efforts. Interestingly enough, Barry also learned a lot about the inner workings of the organization as he discovered why some company practices were causing customers to delay paying bills. He worked to eliminate these issues for customers. All this greatly reduced friction between finance and sales. Barry got the financial information he needed, customer service improved, the organization got its bills paid more promptly, and Barry's career moved forward. It was a true win-win-win-win situation.

- **Make effective group presentations.**

Public speaking and making presentations are tasks that some people consider onerous and even frightening. However, public speaking is a critical skill that gets attention within and outside an organization. Resources for developing this skill are discussed in the Skills section of this book. Here's a Real-World Experience of how it can help you get noticed:

Real-World Experience
<u>Stepping forward to speak</u>

I was fresh out of college and one year into a position with a major corporation that manufactured and sold large industrial equipment. I had been largely unnoticed by senior management when a major trade show was scheduled. Noticing no one had stepped forward to create and perform booth presentations, I volunteered. This was seen as difficult, somewhat undesirable work, involving several presentations each hour for eight hours each day in the show booth.

Public speaking was one of my skills, and I drew on this to prepare and perform the presentations. In the final rehearsal, all of the company's senior managers showed up unannounced to watch my presentation (mainly to make sure that I wouldn't screw it up). This gave me instant exposure to managers who had been previously oblivious to me. It went very well. Then, when doing the presentations at the trade show, I was noticed by other leaders in the industry. This propelled me to a promotion and an invitation to do several additional presentations – and effectively launched my career in this industry.

- **Write reports (whether asked to or not) that are easy to read.**

In a time when face-to-face meetings can be difficult due to geography or schedules, reports often become an important communication tool, particularly when it comes to reaching people you can't meet, or whom you meet on rare occasions. Writing is discussed in more detail in the Skills section of this book, but here's an example of where effective writing paid off to advance a career.

Real-World Experience

<u>Taking the initiative</u>

Carrie was new to the sales organization of a major corporation. Her initial assignment was to visit distributors around the country, carrying the organization's message. While she wasn't asked to do this, after each visit she wrote a simple trip report and submitted it to her supervisor. The outline of the report included:

- *Trip Details*
- *Trip Objectives*
- *Executive Summary (never more than one page)*
- *Observations*
- *Specific recommendations to improve that distributor's performance as well as recommendations for changes in her company's practices to help that distributor and distributors in general*

Carrie's supervisor was impressed and passed the reports up the management ladder. This drew positive attention to the supervisor and Carrie. Her perspectives and recommendations traveled to executives she had never met. Her succinct, to-the-point style was appreciated. She was next asked to research and write a special report on competition. The report included:

- *Report Objectives*
- *Methodology*
- *Executive Summary (including comparisons of her company with key competitors in a spreadsheet)*
- *Details on each competitor*
- *Recommendations to position the company's strategies vis-à-vis competitors*
- *Appendix with backup material*

The report was so well received that it made it to the CEO of the company, who asked Carrie to make a special verbal presentation to the board, summarizing the report. Carrie was again noticed and her career began to accelerate.

- **Use humor appropriately.**

Humor is not joke-telling. The elements of organizational humor are discussed more completely in the Skills section of this book. Here's an example of how the appropriate use of humor reflected positively on Jack and on his career.

Real-World Experience

<u>*Not your boring PowerPoint*</u>

Jack was appointed to give a presentation at the end of a weeklong sales conference. Everyone was tired and anticipating a boring sales summary followed by a "rah rah" closing. Instead, using PowerPoint slides of scenes from old-time movies, Jack gave a thirty-minute "highlights" of the week, projecting company personalities onto the slides in a gently kidding, humorous way. He infused self-deprecation into the mix using "pictures" of himself riding an elephant (leading the sales charge) and being "assaulted" by the Marx Brothers (representing competitors).

At the end of his presentation, Jack got a standing ovation. This humorous speech was talked about for years. Jack was often kidded about the elephant…but he was definitely noticed and remembered in a good way. He further developed this concept for use in other organizations. It was always well received and always got Jack noticed positively.

Get Started

1. Identify the unique skills or knowledge that you can use to quickly and positively impact the organization, but which may not have been acknowledged or utilized yet by the organization.

2. Put together a one-page plan for using these skills effectively in the organization.

3. Ask for time to present this to a person who can act on it.

HOW TO POSITIVELY IMPACT MEETINGS YOU AREN'T CHAIRING

The Overview

One key to positively impacting an organization is to conduct effective meetings. The next How-to chapter contains specifics for doing that. However, when you first join an organization, you will more likely be invited to attend meetings chaired by others.

A quote often attributed to the comedian Woody Allen is "Eighty percent of success is showing up." The message is that it's difficult to impact a meeting if you don't show up.

Deciding whether or not to attend is your first important decision regarding meetings. If you decide not to attend a meeting you are invited to, let the person convening the meeting know in advance. If appropriate, discuss why you are not attending. This alone may positively impact future similar meetings as it can reveal what makes this sort of meeting more desirable or "attendable" (that's another word I made up).

Following are practices and strategies for "making a difference"…a noticeable positive impact…in meetings you attend but don't chair. Because such meetings may often be your initial interface with senior members of an organization, positively impacting such meetings is another way to get early positive notice in an organization. Many of the meeting strategies and tactics outlined here apply to meetings you attend in person as well as those you attend electronically. However, meetings you attend via conference call, individual "call in," or videoconferencing require additional special techniques and skills for you to positively impact. These are specifically discussed in the final bullet point of this chapter.

The Details

- **Do your homework before the meeting. Review the pre-meeting information provided. Ask questions before the meeting.**

Don't go to a meeting uninformed or unprepared. Sometimes the most important meeting work is done before the meeting by asking questions about agenda items or reports (email is excellent for this); by reading reference material distributed before the meeting; and by connecting with people to discuss agenda items before the meeting. Meetings often confirm what the leaders have already decided. If you aren't part of the pre-meeting process, your impact on the meeting and its issues will most likely be limited.

- **Show up a little early.**

Arriving late to a meeting gets the wrong kind of attention. You may miss the opening comments, which often frame a meeting, or you may lose the meeting flow. You may also find yourself asking questions that were answered earlier when you weren't there (that always makes you look silly). When you are early, you can focus your attention on the agenda and any supplemental materials supplied at that time, and perhaps ask a question or two of the leader if he or she is also early. When you are early you may have an opportunity to chat with fellow participants as they arrive, before the meeting starts. This is a great time to connect for building personal, professional relationships, or clarifying any agenda-related questions. Some of your most effective meeting time can be in those few casual minutes before the meeting starts. You may also have some of these informal conversations after a meeting ends, but people often scatter quickly after meetings, and you miss this opportunity.

- **Seat yourself strategically.**

By being early you may have the option of choosing your seat. Give yourself a good view of the room and any audiovisual screens. Sit where you can connect with others. If you plan to leave early, sit near the exit.

- **Don't be distracted with personal electronic devices during the meeting.**

Texting, reading emails, or otherwise interfacing with electronic devices is disrespectful and causes you to lose the flow of the meeting. You may be called on to respond when you aren't ready or when you don't even know the question! Focusing on personal electronic devices during the meeting (other than referring to meeting-related documents or taking notes) indicates you are unengaged in the meeting – and it's a turnoff to others. If the stuff happening outside the meeting is more important than the meeting, stay away from the meeting.

- **Pay attention to what's happening and always ask yourself "What's really going on here? What went on before the meeting that's influencing what's happening now? Is the meeting accomplishing its objectives? Why or why not?"**

Many meetings have subtexts taking place that aren't on the agenda. These include the playing out of interactions that have taken place before the meeting, behind the scenes, or between participants. In many cases, these interactions involve issues that should be discussed more openly, but aren't for whatever reason. They may involve power struggles or relationship issues between members of the organization. As the meeting progresses, work to understand who is jockeying for position; who has an ax to grind; who is maneuvering; who is avoiding responsibility; what is being finessed; who is showing real leadership; what is not being discussed but perhaps should be; what is being discussed but seems a waste of time or irrelevant.

- **Ask pertinent, open-ended questions. Listen to the answers. Ask appropriate follow-up questions.**

One of the most impressive things you can do as a participant in a meeting is to ask relevant, revealing questions that direct the discussion. People often respect perceptive questions in a meeting more than speeches. Honest, open-ended questions are the most effective. That is, questions that begin with who, what, why, how, when, where. "Why do we think customer complaints are increasing?" "Who is in charge of the move into the new facility?" "Why do we think revenue has dropped for three straight months?" This is an important way for newer members of organizations to insert themselves in the discussion in an intelligent, effective, noticeable way.

- **Offer a few thoughtful, informed comments relevant to the discussion, but do more asking and listening than talking.**

See previous bullet point.

- **Take notes.**

Taking notes makes you look like you're engaged. More important, it actually helps keep you engaged! Taking notes will help you remember stuff after the meeting. Of course this can be done on paper, electronic devices, or via another method.

- **If it is the kind of meeting where votes are taken, call for votes when the conversation is apparently exhausted.**

When meetings involve votes, the discussion often drags on way too long. Participants – and meeting leaders – often appreciate a simple call for the vote when discussion points are being repeated, no fresh information is surfacing, one person begins to dominate the floor, or there are other indications it's time to make a decision. If the meeting does not have a formal voting protocol, but it is obvious a decision needs to be made, you can work to bring that to a head at an appropriate time, with comments like, "Have we reached a decision here?" "Should we move forward with that plan?"

"Are we in consensus on that decision?" "Summarizing what I believe we've agreed upon.... Should we move forward?"

- **Volunteer for something appropriate.**

Doing this makes you look good, gives you experience, and makes stuff happen.

- **Quickly follow up on any commitments you make in the meeting.**

Follow-up and follow-through are always noticed and respected, because many people don't follow-up, follow-through or respond in a timely manner

- **Special instructions for electronic meetings or for participating electronically.**

Circumstances arise where you cannot physically be in the meeting room, but you want or need to attend. Or, you may be invited to attend an "all-electronic" meeting (i.e., a conference call in which everyone participates by phone or video or other electronic medium). Occasionally, an issue requiring a vote may be handled strictly by email, without the meeting.

When calling in via phone, it is more difficult to have an impact than in either in-person meetings or videoconferencing. You aren't seen. You may have a natural reluctance to interject yourself into the discussion. You may not be clear who is in the meeting. The meeting technology may not be top quality, making it difficult to hear or participate verbally. It is more difficult to interject since you aren't being seen and can't see the body language of others. As a call-in participant, you may not have access to all of the video and/or the handouts, particularly those inserted into the meeting at the last minute.

Be sure you have accurate call-in information and time for the call. I've seen participants miss a meeting simply by not compensating for time zone differences. Try to obtain handouts or visuals electronically ahead of time.

Remember to be on time. Some call-in systems time out if no one is on the line, and it will be difficult to identify yourself after the meeting starts. Some conference call systems play music until a caller arrives; this becomes annoying and so the system may be turned off as the meeting starts, thus eliminating your opportunity to participate. When you call in late, no one may notice that you're there, so it becomes even more difficult for you to participate.

Try to call in from a quiet, private place. In phone conferencing, you may mute your phone to avoid ancillary noise in your area or from your phone causing nuisance noise in the meeting. If you mute, then forget to "unmute" your phone when ready to talk, this causes confusion. And if you think your phone is muted, but it isn't…this can also lead to embarrassing moments.

When calling in to a conference call or meeting, you may be tempted to multitask (text, read stuff, do things unrelated to the discussion, etc.). Avoid this…give the meeting your full attention.

If the leader fails to let call-in participants know who is physically in the meeting and who is calling in, politely interrupt to ask for the other meeting participants to be identified. When you're leaving a call-in meeting while it is still in progress, let the leader know.

When attending a meeting electronically, don't be reluctant to interject with appropriate questions or comments. However, as a call-in participant, you may have to be more verbally assertive since they can't see you indicate you'd like to speak. If you are having trouble hearing other participants, ask for the call volume to be increased or for the equipment to be repositioned. Be sure you speak loudly enough. You may want to be more succinct in a call-in situation since you can't reinforce your comments with visual clues and eye contact, but you do have to interject to participate.

Depending on system quality, videoconferencing offers the opportunity for visual clues and presentations. Most of the electronic tips provided here also apply to videoconferencing. One more important point: Be aware of your background on the video as it may be distracting to others or even send some wrong signals.

With all these complications when calling in to a meeting, it is always easier to positively impact a meeting by being there in person. As Woody Allen said, "Eighty percent of success is showing up."

Real-World Experience

<u>Larry and Warren…two different approaches</u>

Larry always arrived early for meetings. He used the time to greet others, share some humor (often self-deprecating), and ask some pertinent questions in a nonthreatening environment. He looked prepared, with the handouts in front of him either highlighted or marked up with notes he had added for discussion during the meeting.

When new to an organization, Larry was laid back at first, offering a few questions that indicated he had familiarized himself with the key topics.

When discussion of an issue lagged, Larry often called for a vote or summarized a consensus that had developed. Over a long career, Larry was invited to chair every committee, board, and organization he participated in.

When Warren joined a board, he immediately became a "high quantity" speaker. He frequently gave lengthy speeches in which he often repeated himself. He never seemed to do the homework ahead of time, and answers to many of his questions were often in the meeting handouts. Warren frequently prefaced his long statements with "I promised myself I wasn't going to say much this meeting, but…" or "I won't take much time here, but…"

Eyes rolled and participants endured. Few people were persuaded to Warren's point of view because they stopped listening halfway into these harangues. To make it worse, meeting leaders were often not skilled in interrupting and redirecting the discussion, so meetings Warren attended often went on and on, well past the stated end time.

Summarizing their meeting impacts: Less, but informed input (often with questions) in the style of Larry is usually more effective than Warren's lengthy, repetitive style.

Get Started:

1. Make a list of things you see people doing in meetings that actually move the organization forward.

2. Make a list of counterproductive things you see people do in meetings.

3. At your next meeting, ask two pertinent open-ended questions about the topic under consideration. Shut up and listen to the answers. Ask a follow-up question if it seems appropriate.

HOW TO EFFECTIVELY CHAIR MEETINGS

The Overview

A widely quoted estimate of the number of formal meetings in the United States in a year is 11,000,000,000.[1] If that was the number in 1998, you can bet that the number is higher today. Whatever the number, there are a lot of meetings in and between organizations.

When you first start with a new organization, you will be invited to participate in meetings. (See previous chapter, How to Positively Impact Meetings You Don't Run.) You will participate in well-run meetings, and you'll have to endure meetings that are a major waste of time. You can learn a lot about how to effectively chair meetings by observing the mistakes others make in the meetings you wish you weren't in.

The most common complaints about ineffective meetings are:

- Didn't start on time.
- Didn't end on time.
- Took too long (worse than not starting on time).
- No advance notice of critical discussion items.
- Leader wasn't prepared.

---

[1]	A network MCI Conferencing White Paper. Meetings in America: A study of trends, costs and attitudes toward business travel, teleconferencing, and their impact on productivity (Greenwich, CT: INFOCOMM, 1998).

- Nothing was accomplished.
- Someone was allowed to dominate the conversation pointlessly.
- Someone was allowed to distract the meeting in a direction not appropriate for that meeting.
- Overall discussion allowed to ramble without direction.
- Time was spent on stuff that should be handled outside the meeting.
- Person needed to make decisions not there.
- "I wasn't invited."
- Wrong people there.
- "No need for me to be in that meeting."
- Leader assumed certain knowledge on part of attendees, but was wrong.
- Didn't get to critical agenda items.
- "That meeting was scheduled so that it ruined my whole day."
- No follow-up after the meeting.
- Food situation for meeting not handled well.

And perhaps the worst, most easily avoided complaint…
"We didn't need that meeting."

Nothing will kill organizational enthusiasm faster than ineffective meetings. In this chapter I'll walk you through some of the key tips for getting meetings right.

The Details

Planning is an essential part of effective meetings. The first basic questions to ask are:

- Do we really need this meeting?
- What are the objectives of the meeting?
- What are the desired outcomes?

Alternatives to holding meetings include:

- Well-constructed memos to appropriate parties (most likely via email)
- Phone calls and individual conversations with key individuals
- Posting on an intra-organization website or communication platform
- A quick stand-up meeting with the right people
- Discussion over a cup of coffee with the right people
- Skipping a regularly scheduled meeting when there is nothing substantial to be accomplished (most people love getting notice of cancellation of a regularly scheduled meeting for this reason; it's like a gift of time!)
- Increasing the intervals between regularly scheduled meetings (bi-monthly instead of monthly? Quarterly instead of weekly?)

Useful objectives and desired outcomes for meetings in effective organizations can include:

- Get everyone on the same page for a project, initiative, change of plans, event…
- Introduce new members of the organization
- Introduce something new to the organization
- Strategic planning
- Team building
- Detailed planning for a specific project
- Make decisions that require votes (budgets, bylaws, major hiring / firing decision, etc.)
- Training that can't be more effectively done in another format
- Major announcements affecting most members of the organization
- Regular review of progress
- Building confidence in the organization

- Building and maintaining momentum for a project
- Getting different groups in the organization to work together, plan a joint project, work out a disagreement, etc.
- Obtaining feedback on an issue
- Recognition and acknowledgment of performance for individuals, groups within the organization, or the organization itself. Awards! Plaques! Commendations!

Once you've decided to hold a meeting and have a clear idea of its goals, consider these housekeeping items:

- What type of meeting is it? In person? Conference call? In person with call-in capability? Videoconferencing? Use of electronic software meeting tools? The criteria should be: What is the most effective format to accomplish what we need to achieve in this meeting? How will we get key people to participate? What will be the most convenient for the participants?

- If it's an in-person meeting, where will be it held? What facility and room? Factors to consider here include geographic location and access, parking, availability of audiovisual equipment, seating, privacy, noise, susceptibility to interruption, and availability. All of these physical factors can make a meeting effective...or not. These cannot be taken for granted. As mundane as it sounds, putting a meeting in the wrong place or wrong environment can severely, negatively impact attendance and effectiveness.

- What day and time? Consider other people's schedules, access to location, even issues like traffic patterns and parking or transit availability for the time and place. If a meeting is voluntary and too difficult to get to or scheduled at an awkward time, people just won't come or they will resent having to attend.

The people questions:

- Who should you invite? Who really needs to be there for the meeting to accomplish its purposes? Who will be offended if they are not invited? Who can make a positive contribution? Who is available at the scheduled time? Should you plan the meeting place and time around key individuals? Should you reschedule if key individuals can't make it? Who does not need to be there but has routinely been invited in the past?

Announce the meeting:

- Announce far enough in advance so attendees can be prepared.

- Create invitations by phone, email, or other tools that experience shows are most effective for the desired participants. Multiple invitations or reminders may be required in some situations.

- Be sure all pertinent details are with the announcement, including date, time (start time *and* end time), place, special facility instructions or directions, and call-in information (if applicable).

- If using electronic announcements such as Outlook, or document tools such as Dropbox or Go To Meeting, be sure that everyone invited has access to these tools.

- Let everyone know who else is invited to eliminate surprises and facilitate any appropriate pre-meeting conversations.

- Ask for acknowledgments of those planning to attend, or regrets from those who can't attend.

- If people critical to the objectives of the meeting can't attend, consider rescheduling.

- Scheduling meetings to meet individuals' other priorities and schedules is one of the most difficult parts of some meetings. There are several software tools available for productive scheduling: Doodles is one. Search "software for meeting scheduling" to find many more. Use these (when appropriate) for larger numbers of people.

- If appropriate and necessary for a productive meeting, send out critical documents to be reviewed ahead of time. Email attachments and software such as Dropbox are ideal for this, unless some members of the organization don't have access to these tools.

Get prepared for the meeting:

- Create and distribute an agenda prior to the meeting. The person setting the meeting agenda is essentially framing and directing the discussion. This is a powerful tool in the hands of the meeting leader. Email is excellent for distributing agendas ahead of the meeting.. Include expected outcomes. Ask for agenda input and respond by either changing the agenda or explaining why that's not appropriate for this meeting.

- Create any supporting audiovisual tools that you'll need.

- Ask others who may be presenting what audiovisual equipment or tools they need.

- Carefully plan audiovisual equipment needs for compatibility, operator comfort in using them, and anything else that can go wrong and ruin the meeting. Make no assumptions in this area

- Many meetings are called to confirm decisions or arrangements already made outside of the meetings. If there are contentious issues or key issues to be voted on, it is often best to have discussions with key people before the meeting. Find out ahead of time what objections are, how key individuals feel about the issue, how the discussion will probably go, how individuals may vote. This will help the meeting go more smoothly.

In the time immediately before the meeting:

- Arrive early.

- Review arrangements in the room, including seating, potential distractions, lighting, noise, temperature, or anything that could distract from the effectiveness of the meeting.

- If there is something you didn't expect or don't like, make every effort to change it before the meeting starts. It's your meeting, so own it.

- Double-check A/V equipment early enough in advance of the meeting to make adjustments if necessary. Meeting attendee patience for A/V that doesn't work is approximately zero.

- If you're using an agenda, hand it out early.

- Review and prepare other handouts. Note: If you are not referring to the handout immediately, it is more effective to hold it and distribute it when you are ready to discuss it. Premature review of handouts by meeting participants is distracting, causes attendees to lose focus, and can even give some the feeling they have "permission" to leave early (i.e., I've got the information, so I can leave).

- Greet attendees arriving early and, as time permits, engage in informal conversation with them. Begin to build the desired meeting atmosphere. If there are last-minute private conversations that need to take place relative to the meeting, take those persons aside and have those conversations.

Opening the meeting:

- Call the meeting to order as close to the published starting time as possible, realizing that you may want to delay the start time for no more than five minutes if key participants are running late. Let the attendees who are on time know this so they understand the late start. Late starts are basically not good, but they may be necessary for meeting effectiveness.

- Thank attendees for coming.

- Briefly state the objective of the meeting. Highlight the important things that should be accomplished by the end of the meeting. Review the agenda with the group; reconfirm the time you plan to adjourn.

- For smaller groups where time permits, make introductions (or ask for self-introductions) for individuals who don't know each other or who may be new to the organization, or guests. Ask not only for names, but also what their relationship is to the organization and to the topic being discussed. "Let's go around the room (including electronic attendees) and state your name, relationship to the organization, and what you are most interested in seeing accomplished today, or what specific questions you have" (or something else that's appropriate).

Getting others talking early, even with simple introductions, breaks the ice.

- Preview any major decisions or discussions to be had.

"Today, among other matters, it is important we review, discuss, and approve next year's budget; and vote on the nomination of a new member of our board of directors."

During the meeting:

From here, the course of the meeting depends on its purpose, number of attendees, and other elements specific to the meeting. However, here are some general tips on conducting effective meetings:

- If a certain level of knowledge on the meeting's subject is critical, or when there are new members of the group, one of the most effective things a meeting leader can do is search out the least level of knowledge in the room for that subject, and then do a quick summary to bring everyone up to date (or up to the level required for productive discussion). Meeting leaders frequently miss this step resulting in some attendees getting "lost" early in discussions because their knowledge level was mistakenly assumed to be more than it is.

- Where the meetings involve attendee discussions, you must keep it moving while allowing for appropriate input from those who need or want to give input.

- Use open-ended questions to direct and redirect the meeting discussion. "Who has questions on the budget?" or "How can we address this problem?"

- Do not let one person dominate or take the meeting into irrelevant territory. This means you must be prepared to politely (but firmly) interrupt. "Larry, I appreciate your input. Brenda, what is your view of that?" "Who has input on this?" "Thanks, Bill. Who has a response to that?" "We've heard a lot of discussion on this and probably can't reach a decision today…let's defer this to a smaller group outside this meeting, to report back later." Failure to do this can and will destroy a meeting's effectiveness.

- On the other hand, it is also important to continually observe everyone in the meeting, looking for individuals who should be giving input but aren't. Or whose facial expressions indicate dissatisfaction or disagreement. You need to draw those people into the discussion. "George, we haven't heard from you; what is your view of this idea?" Failure to do this may lead to missed points, or worse, leave an objection unvoiced (that objection will inevitably fester and surface outside the meeting, often to the detriment of the organization). Skilled meeting facilitators are constantly observing individuals, cutting short conversation dominators, and drawing in those who are not participating. You may even need to use a closed-ended question with someone who has been objecting but whose cooperation you need. "Linda, can you live with this approach? Will you support this? Do you have other objections we haven't dealt with?"

- If major dissension surfaces in verbal arguments, it may be necessary to adjourn and work on this topic outside of the meeting. It is the facilitator's responsibility to sense when this is necessary to avoid destructive comments, and to then take action.

- Maintain awareness of time. Even more important than starting on time, people will often judge the success of a meeting by it ending on time. If you feel the meeting must run past the scheduled time in order to accomplish objectives, ask for consensus to do this and then estimate a new end time. If key people can't stay, consider adjourning and reconvening at a later time.

At the end of the meeting:

- Clearly summarize any important actions taken, make a call for appropriate follow-up action, announce the time and place for any follow-up or regularly scheduled meeting, and thank attendees for coming.

"Today we solidified plans for the new product introduction and made specific assignments for implementation. You have printed and electronic copies of the time line and responsibilities. Is anyone unclear on their responsibility? Thanks for coming. Our next progress meeting is 8:30 on September 5 in this room. Let's make it happen!"

After the meeting:

- Another effective tool in the hands of the meeting leader is to distribute a summary of meeting discussion, decisions, or follow-up activities. Just as creating the agenda frames the meeting discussion, the after meeting summary can frame "next steps".

- Promptly follow up on any actions committed to or required as a result of the meeting. This is critical to the meeting's success, and to the attendance and success of any additional meetings of this group.

- Communicate this follow-up succinctly and clearly to all attendees and to anyone who is impacted by the meeting – whether they attended or not.

When you hold a primarily in-person meeting that includes call-in participants:

- Distribute call-in information well in advance of the meeting (and make sure it works).

- Ask telephone attendees to let you know they will be calling in.

- Email handouts or other visuals (such as PowerPoint presentations) to call-in attendees sometime before the meeting starts and let them know you are doing this so they can come to the meeting prepared.

- Be sure equipment to receive calls in the meeting room is set, ready to go and working. As basic as it sounds, often this is a missing piece. Everything is queued up and the call-in phone is not working or no one knows how to work it. If the call-in speaker equipment is not working, cell phones with speaker can be used, but often these have poor audio quality.

- Ask attendees to identify themselves as they join the call for the meeting. Keep notes on who has joined so you don't forget.

- When the meeting starts, let those who are calling in know who is in the room, and let those in the room know who is calling in.

- Call-in attendees are often reluctant to interrupt the conversation and join in. At appropriate points, overtly ask for their input.

- If confidential voting is taking place in the meeting, make some arrangement for an appropriate person to take the votes privately.

Special note about food in meetings:

Providing food for meetings introduces a number of potentially complicating factors:

- Is everyone aware ahead of time that there will be food and what it will be?

- Who will be responsible to prepare or arrange for it? Get it there? Pay for it?

- What should it be? The old donuts standby doesn't fit well with today's health-conscious population. Many people have diet restrictions or preferences that must be accommodated.

- If allowing attendees to order food ahead of time, who manages the process?

- Where should you eat it? If at the meeting tables, food produces a mess and drinks could potentially damage electronics. If another room, is that reserved?

- Should you take a break to "do" food? Will it be served, or should people just get up and help themselves whenever they are ready, potentially breaking the meeting's focus?

- What do you do with the trash?

- What do you do with the leftover food?

- Who cleans up?

- Anticipate stated or unstated complaints from people who don't like the food.

Here's some advice on food and meetings:

- Avoid it if you can; it's a lot of trouble. This means paying attention to meeting schedule time versus conventional eating schedules. You can avoid food for most meetings two hours or less if you provide appropriate beverages such as water, coffee, or juice. Just be sure to let people know there will not be food.

- If it's an early morning meeting, you can provide pre-packaged food if you must (granola bars, etc.), along with beverages.

- If taking a break during the meeting to eat, try to move to an adjoining area where the mess can be contained, and folks can enjoy building relationships instead of eating while trying to participate in the meeting.

- If the meeting is centered on a meal (i.e., a fund-raising breakfast, a "working" lunch, dinner after the meeting, etc.) let people know ahead of time what will be served and give them options to accommodate diet restrictions. Take a break from the meeting agenda to allow dining and conversation. Then bring the meeting back to order with greater focus on the business at hand.

Real-World Experience

<u>Bad experiences</u>

Within just the last year I have seen the effectiveness of meetings compromised by a variety of problems. For example:

- *First meeting agenda item was "review and approve the organization's budget." The meeting facilitator did not bring a copy of the budget. The meeting was delayed while it was found and copied.*

- *Facilitator used a flipchart, but had narrow, small pointed markers instead of larger, broad, felt tip markers. No one could read what was on the chart.*

- *Leader couldn't get computer to talk to projector. Meeting delayed ten minutes while tech guy was summoned. Some attendees left before the meeting started.,*

- *Evening meeting, scheduled to adjourn about 6:30. Someone went to a lot of trouble to supply food. Attendees not notified ahead of time, so they made other plans. No one ate the food.*

- *Evening meeting scheduled for ninety minutes lasted three hours because leader was reluctant to cut off speakers who rambled. Several attendees left before meeting ended, due to other commitments, impatience, and hunger! Dinner was to be served afterward. Kitchen staff was upset. The meal was cold.*

- *Five of the organization's staff members were forced to come to monthly board meetings but never asked to give a report. Several topics discussed were inappropriate for staff members.*

- *Leader at board meeting called for dismissal of executive director. Several board members left angry because it had not been announced that this would be on the agenda, causing a major organizational rift.*

- *Leader opened meeting by apologizing for not being prepared…but went ahead with meeting anyway and stumbled through agenda. Probably should have cancelled ahead of start time.*

- *Person began statement by saying "I won't need more than five minutes…'" then rambled on for twenty minutes, boring everyone in the room. Meeting leader didn't understand how to stop it.*

- *Leader began meeting assuming everyone there knew the problem being addressed and the terminology used. Several didn't. They were frustrated and eventually stopped the meeting to "catch up", frustrating others.*

You probably have your own meeting horror stories. Learn from them.

Get Started

1. Make a list of things meeting leaders do that make the meeting less effective.

2. Look for an opportunity to fill in for a meeting leader who can't be at a scheduled meeting, or to convene a meeting on a relevant topic.

3. Don't do any of the things on your list of ineffective meeting leader actions!

HOW TO SELL YOUR IDEAS IN YOUR ORGANIZATION

The Overview

A complaint often overheard among members of organizations:

"They don't ever listen to my ideas." This can be understood to mean "I can't sell my ideas."

Simply suggesting ideas doesn't make them happen. They have to be sold. Then, they have to be implemented.

Selling ideas in an organization means:

- Helping the right people understand how your ideas will benefit the organization as a whole.
- Overcoming objections to the ideas.
- Competing successfully with alternative ideas put forward by others.
- Overcoming organization inertia.
- Convincing the right people that the ideas can actually be implemented and are worth the effort and cost.
- Successfully implementing the idea(s) – if you are ever going to sell another one!

Put simply, it's about *selling*.

There are generally three audiences for selling ideas in an organization:

- Selling ideas to your supervisors or organization leaders (aka *selling up*);

- As team leader, selling ideas to your team (so they enthusiastically help you hone and implement them); and

- Generally, selling ideas within an organization in a way that ensures that those ideas take hold and come to fruition.

The basic principles and skills of selling ideas are the same in all three situations, but the approaches can vary. These principles and skills are outlined below... along with some of the situational variations.

The Details

For relatively simple ideas with non-complex implementation, and in a relatively flat organization, you may not need to take all of the steps outlined below to sell your idea. In some small or volunteer organizations, for example, a simple dose of enthusiasm and a willingness to take responsibility for the implementation can get the idea sold. This is particularly true for ideas that don't involve much money or organizational risk.

However, the more impactful the ideas, the higher the cost, risk, and complexity of implementation; the more complex and hierarchal the organization, the more of these idea-selling elements come into play.

Part of the skill of selling is determining how much effort and which skills and tactics to employ in selling your ideas. What's it worth? What's the potential payoff? Let's discuss some of these elements in more detail:

Enthusiasm can be a key ingredient in selling anything — especially ideas. It indicates your level of belief in the idea, and potentially your willingness to help implement it. Enthusiasm can be contagious.

A good idea is only good if it can be shown to *benefit the organization*. Your ability to complete this sentence is key: "This idea will improve the organization by…"

The more specific the articulation of benefit, the easier the sell. What *homework* have you done? Do you have numbers, examples, testimonials, or other "proof" of potential benefits? Where has this concept worked well in other organizations? The process of selling ideas essentially comes down to convincing the right people at the right time that the benefits of a new idea to the organization are worth the implementation costs and trouble.

Your good idea may benefit the organization, but it may also negatively impact some constituents. Maybe it will create more work for them, or lower their status, or violate the way they think things should work. Considering how your idea affects others (i.e., empathy) will alert you to the potential *objections* that you may have to deal with. It may also trigger your need to approach these individuals separately before the idea goes public, adjusting the idea per their recommendations and *pre-selling* the idea to key people.

When it comes to selling ideas, *allies* are always better than enemies. Quietly testing the idea out on interested stakeholders inside and outside the organization can help build support before you are ready to sell it to the organization as a whole.

A willingness to *negotiate* details or even major parts of your idea may help sell it. Your idea may not be perfect as presented, and by discussing it with others you may learn how to improve it. This is called collaboration. Even if your idea is perfect, it may not be sellable to the organization without being negotiated. Accepting others' thoughts or modifications to your ideas will also help develop support and allies for the idea. It's now *their* idea as well as *yours*.

You will want to consider the *appropriate time* to introduce your new idea. If the organization and/or the individuals who need to be sold are in the throes of closing out the year-end, involved in a seasonal rush, dealing with a crisis, or managing other distractions, it may be better to wait. Ideas involving major change, for example, may be best sold during the organization's regular budgeting or other planning cycle.

Personal considerations of the decision makers also come into play. If key people are out of town, getting ready for vacation, or dealing with other personal factors that might hinder full consideration, it may be more effective for you to wait for better timing. Even time of the week or day can be a factor. For example, on Monday mornings organizations are often getting their bearings after a weekend – not necessarily a good time to break new ground. The same can be said for Friday afternoons, when activities are wrapping up for the weekend.

Creating a document outlining the benefits, costs, challenges, implementation steps for an idea helps frame the discussion…and give credibility to the idea. One example and one template for this are given later in this chapter.

If the idea must be presented to a group in a meeting setting, your *presentation skills* can be important in selling the idea. (See the Skills section of this book for recommendations on developing presentation and public speaking skills).

When selling an idea, it helps to include *implementation* plans, schedules and costs, as well as any risks of failure. This illustrates a well-thought-through idea and builds confidence that the idea is viable and can be implemented. It also gives you and the organization a running start when the idea is approved. If the person presenting the idea is willing to accept responsibility for implementation, that can serve as a powerful part of selling the idea. If you get approval as well as responsibility for implementation, you have more control over its ultimate success. Nothing sells the next idea like a previous idea's success!

Selling ideas in an organization can be hard work. It takes planning, listening, relationship building, negotiating, timing, presenting, and implementing. But selling ideas in an organization is a lot more effective than lamenting, "They just don't listen to me."

Real-World Experience

The Golf Tournament

Vice President of Sales Loren had a great idea. He approached the company president as he was getting ready to go home one day in November and exclaimed enthusiastically: "I think we should have a company golf tournament for customers!"

On his way out the door, the president simply said: "I've been to a couple of those and they just looked like a waste of time to me. See you tomorrow."

Loren had violated several rules of selling ideas: Timing for presenting the idea was bad; it was the end of the day and the end of golf season. He stated no benefits for the company and had no plan for implementation. There were two other vice presidents of sales in the company in different areas, and neither of them had joined him to present the idea. He had no implementation plan and no idea of cost. The president liked to consider ideas in writing rather than offhand verbal interfaces.

Realizing his mistake, Loren regrouped. He got the other two vice presidents together and discussed the idea. They quickly bought in, with some concept improvements developed in their discussions.

They visited a golf course known for hosting successful customer events, and connected with the course's experienced event advisor. He related key elements of successful customer tournaments of similar organizations, and several of these elements were incorporated into the tournament plan for their company.

The vice presidents of sales then put together a two-page document recommending the idea. The outline of the report was:

- **A Customer Golf Tournament...Signature Marketing Event for Our Company!** *(note the enthusiasm)*

- **Measureable Benefits for Our Company** (these included significant time with customer decision influencers to build personal, professional relationships; visibility and time with key suppliers who would sponsor the event; catalysts to call on customers and treat them special while inviting them — whether they come or not...)

- **Timeline**

- **Details** (included how many customers to be invited; form of invitations; what golf course; which suppliers to invite; type of competition for the tournament, etc.)

- **Budget** (included cost remediation through selling sponsorships to suppliers who would be invited)

- **Supporting documentation** (testimonials from other companies which had held similar tournaments)

They invited the president to a meeting at the golf club (away from office distractions and in the event environment) along with the club's event advisor, who showed the president around, including viewing pictures of other events held there. After the vice presidents presented their report, they left the club with approval and responsibility to make it happen.

The president now was so enthused about the possibilities that he contributed ideas, budget money, and a personal effort to the cause. He in turn helped sell the event to salespeople who would invite customers and also to suppliers who would help fund it. The president made a special presentation to the company's chief financial officer (CFO) so he would know the story and not later question individual expenses of the event, without knowing the event details and benefits to the company. In other words, the president, after being sold, resold the idea to the CFO recruiting him as an "ally" to help make the tournament a success. The CFO was invited to join the salespeople, customers, and suppliers at the event. The customer golf event, initially rejected as a bad idea, became an annual signature marketing event for the company. The idea had been "sold." At least twice.

The Partners

When I took a senior management position at a company owned jointly by two partners, I looked at the organization chart and saw Jack was president and Bob was secretary-treasurer. I was told that when I had major ideas to recommend, I should run them by Jack…which seemed to make sense as he was president.

However, I also heard from employees that when they took their ideas to Jack, he often said "Yes." Then, nothing seemed to happen. It turned out Jack then took the ideas to his partner Bob. Bob had not initially been involved in the discussions and had heard the sales pitch for the ideas secondhand from Jack. Bob asked a lot of pertinent questions that the individuals who proposed the ideas were not there to answer. As a result, ideas and action languished.

I decided to try a different approach. I learned that to sell ideas to the partners, I should take the ideas to both Bob and Jack at the same time, in a joint meeting. I discovered the best time of day to do this was about 9:30 AM, when everyone was fresh, and after the partners had their informal morning review of issues over coffee together in the break room. It was often effective to give them a heads-up about the meeting topic prior to the meeting so they could think things over and be ready with their questions. If one of the partners unexpectedly could not be in the meeting, I almost always rescheduled it. It was that important to meet with both partners together.

I came to these meetings prepared with written recommendations, occasionally providing these ahead of time, but I learned that the best communication style for Bob and Jack was a verbal presentation followed by their questions and mutual discussion. My goal was to come out of the meetings with the okay to move ahead and with the authority to make it happen. If one or both of the partners brought up strong objections that I had not anticipated; if there was further information needed for a decision or if they suggested improvements to the concept, requiring major modifications, we adjourned the meeting and reconvened when we had answers or a revised proposal. I took the initiative to convene the follow-up meetings. Often we worked collaboratively in the meetings to improve the ideas and recommendations, and I was then given authority and responsibility to proceed *immediately. Occasionally we decided in these meetings to kill an idea. It most likely needed killing. Good decisions were made and implemented in this manner for the more than twenty years we worked together.*

I also came to understand that if my ideas were not major, a more effective way to sell them was during that morning coffee the partners usually enjoyed together. I would join them after they convened, and have coffee with them while sharing organizational news, offering a little humor, and getting their okay on a relatively minor idea or decision.

Resource

<u>A template to help sell your ideas</u>

Here's a template I've used to sell major ideas. This can be used for written or oral presentation of ideas, and should be modified as appropriate for the situation. Of course this should be used in conjunction with all the other idea-selling principles discussed in this chapter.

<XYZ> Project Proposal

(Give your project a name to elevate it in everyone's minds)

- Current situation triggering need for this recommendation
- Alternatives considered to deal with this
- The recommendation (simply stated, with relevant details following here or in an appendix)
- Benefits to the organization
- Implementation: who should be responsible, costs, timelines
- Risks of failure (what's the downside, if any?)
- Issues to be dealt with (these are objections you've uncovered in doing your homework, and how you are dealing with them)

- Next steps if approved

- Appendix with alternative proposals (if warranted), drawings, and anything else that's needed and shows you did your homework (but could have distracted from your presentation if handed out earlier)

Modify this template for your situation. Whether you use this exact template or not, be sure to consider these elements when making your case to sell an idea in or to an organization.

Get Started:

1. Write down an idea you'd like to sell to your organization.

2. Write down three ways that your idea will benefit the organization.

3. Identify the key people who need to be sold and who might oppose it.

4. Get started selling the idea using the concepts in this section. Creating a "selling document" is one great way to start.

HOW TO DEVELOP WORKING RELATIONSHIPS WITH FINANCE/ACCOUNTING AND WHY IT'S IMPORTANT

The Overview

Individuals who have finance/accounting responsibilities within their respective organizations usually have influence beyond their position on the organization chart. Through their reporting, budgeting, interpretation of reports, cash management, and banking relationships, they provide top management with the information and confidence to move forward (or, a caution to not move forward) with projects. In times of financial crisis, finance managers may control the organization's destiny.

On a more everyday basis, finance and accounting professionals influence and manage budgets; have major input into employee issues such as pay and benefits; review expense reporting; and manage capital investments. They impact customers through billing and collection practices. Eventually, finance and accounting touch and impact every aspect of most ongoing organizations. Yet newer members of organizations who are not in these fields often ignore them. One reason is that they may not have ever been introduced to the finance team, or perhaps they were introduced only superficially. Sometimes the introduction is made with a joke like, "Don't upset these guys or you won't get your paycheck, ha, ha, ha."

It's a good idea to circle back and meet the finance and accounting crew on a more serious level, to establish personal, professional relationships.

An important thing to remember is that most of these professionals don't want to be thought of as just "bean counters" (an unfortunate slang phrase sometimes used for accounting and finance people). They want to, and usually do, play integral roles in the organization's strategies and tactics. When you acknowledge their important roles and involve them early and often in your organization work, you gain their respect and build personal, professional relationships that will benefit both you and the organization.

The Details

Methods of forming effective working relationships with accounting and finance (personal, professional relationships) are similar to forming these relationships elsewhere in the organization...but often must be more intentional and with some variations specific to finance areas:

- Get to know them by asking open-ended questions about their background, responsibilities, and challenges. Learn something of their story.

- Share your story, including education, job history, goals in working for this organization, challenges you face.

- Don't disparage or work around their procedures. Work with them or suggest appropriate changes in their procedures, with clear delineation of benefits of these changes to the organization and its financial health.

- Be circumspect about the organization's money (this is a good idea for many reasons).

- Don't abuse personal expense accounts. If you are a poor steward of the organization's money in this area, it will be assumed you are not a good steward in other areas.

- Learn the basics of reading financial reports (See Skills section of this book).

- Ask meaningful questions about the financial and accounting reports.

- Answer their questions about expense or other financial items seriously with appropriate explanations.

- Don't simply ask for funds or give receipts for extraordinary expense items or "blow off" budget overruns. Take time to seek out finance / accounting people involved and explain what's going on. Tell them the story.

- Get finance and accounting involved early in projects involving major capital expenditures. It's repetitive, but tell them the story about how this project will benefit the organization. See "How to Sell Your Ideas."

Real-World Experience

Sales, accounting partnership pays off

Two years into a new job, I was assigned the responsibility of selling (i.e., disposing of) excess inventory of a failed product line. Worse, the equipment involved had been stored outdoors and had significantly deteriorated. Unfortunately, it was still on the books at original inflated values minus token depreciation. It simply could not be sold at the values stated in the accounting records, and accounting controlled those values. Management was reluctant to sell the equipment at a loss (i.e., below book value).

I faced a dilemma. How could I sell this equipment when the pricing didn't reflect the equipment condition or market for it?

I decided to seek out the accounting employee who was in charge of maintaining inventory values to see what I could learn and to ask for help. That person was Arnold, and he had never actually seen the equipment involved — even before deterioration. For him, the equipment and its values were numbers on a page.

I decided to ask for help from and work with Arnold instead of trying to override his valuations. I learned he had been with the company for almost his entire 25-year career. Of course he took great pride in his work, but felt somewhat marginalized by marketing, sales, and engineering departments.

I took time to explain the sales problem with the equipment, then invited Arnold on a visit to a dealer to see the inventory. Arnold had never visited a dealer before. It was an eye opener as he talked to dealer salespeople about the equipment and then inspected it in its deteriorated state.

Arnold began to understand the problem beyond just the numbers. Back at the office, he found a reserve account in which he could write off the equipment's inventory costs so it could have a book value truly reflecting its value (i.e., at a price at which the equipment could actually be sold).

I went to work selling the equipment – always involving Arnold in the story of each sale. It became the two of us as a team, helping the company clean up this mess. As long as I was at the company, Arnold was on my team and helped make things happen that might not have otherwise happened. It was a true personal, professional relationship benefiting the organization.

<u>The CFO who was more than that</u>

The organization was a nonprofit. Its revenue primarily involved a complex medical billing process with insurance companies. The clinicians providing the services were not financially oriented, and in some cases resented even talking about money. They were focused on serving the patients.

The board of directors had recently accepted the resignation of its executive director (ED), who had clashed with some of the staff due to his management style focusing on some of the financial issues of the organization. Key clinicians had left or were planning to leave. The organization was at risk of collapsing. The new ED immediately met with the CFO and realized she was the key to the organization's short-term survival. The ED and CFO quickly formed a personal, professional relationship focused on saving the organization.

The CFO was trusted by the staff, and became a conduit for the ED to feed financial realities to the clinical staff without becoming overbearing or alarming. The CFO joined the ED in sharing the financial story with the staff. She also made the ED aware of employee concerns that required action. She told the "staff story" to the ED. Together they made the difficult decisions required to meet short-term cash requirements while getting the organization stabilized.

Get Started

1. If you don't personally know the financial team in your organization, introduce yourself. Learn something of their story, and share something of yours.

2. Ask them open-ended questions about their job and some of the challenges they are facing.

3. Look for some way within the organization to help them with their challenges.

HOW TO EXHIBIT LEADERSHIP

The Overview

You do not have to be a leader by title or position in order to exhibit effective leadership. Leadership can be exhibited from a position of authority, and/or from most any position in an organization. Leadership in the sense described here is defined as taking the lead in moving the organization forward in a positive direction.

Following is a list of specific things that exhibit leadership. All of the actions encompassed by these bullet points lead to the most important prerequisite required to exhibit leadership that is respected by others in the organization:

Leaders must earn the trust of others in the organization and those who interface with the organization.

The Details

To exhibit leadership and be acknowledged as a leader in organizations, you should:

- Put the organization's interests above your own…and be seen to do this.
- Put the interests of others in the organization above your own.
- Make your actions consistent with your talk. As the cliché says, you should "walk the talk."
- Step up when difficult tasks need to be handled.

- Do your homework before expressing strong opinions.

- Offer positive recommendations, and sell them (see "How to Sell Your Ideas").

- Admit mistakes and don't make excuses. Then, take corrective action.

- Keep a positive attitude and demeanor...even when dealing with negative situations or crises. This doesn't mean ignore real problems... it means after acknowledging the problem, take a "now what can we do to improve things?" attitude.

- Don't engage in negative conversation or gossip about the organization, your supervisors, leaders, or other employees.

- Avoid inappropriate personal entanglements within the organization.

- Follow others when they responsibly take the lead.

- Make decisions when needed.

- Project the organization forward in your mind and share the vision; create a sense of forward motion.

- Communicate clearly.

- Listen more than you talk.

- Make things happen.

- When a crisis presents itself, step forward to take action as appropriate.

- Respect ethical, moral, and legal boundaries.

Real-World Experience

<u>*Starting quietly*</u>

In many instances, starting quietly — exhibiting leadership in a position of non-authority within an organization — naturally transitions to a more formal leadership role.

When I was new with an organization, I used the strategy of starting low-key, doing my homework, asking open-ended questions, forming personal, professional relationships, using humor, and taking advantage of any speaking opportunities, since this was one of my skills.

As I became more familiar with an organization, I proposed, then sold, ideas. I was always circumspect about the organization's money, and got to know the finance professionals in the organization. Where appropriate, I would volunteer for a task considered undesirable.

This initial "leading from behind" approach took me to many top leadership positions in every organization I joined.

Leadership without the title

Judy was executive secretary for several senior company executives. She had their trust and confidence. She also interfaced regularly with most other organization members in the break room, at company social events, and simply around the company with her wide range of responsibilities.

When Judy felt the top executives needed to know something involving the staff, she told them in private without ever breaking employee confidence. Most of her communications were about changes needed to benefit the company and the employees; occasionally she communicated situations that needed to be resolved quickly. She often sold her own ideas — and those of other employees — to management, but without ever appearing to "sell." Judy would also take the time to informally explain the rationale of some management decisions to employees so they would be better understood. She knew how to communicate up and down in the organization. And she held everyone's trust since she never advocated for her own personal benefit. Over many years, Judy's quiet leadership helped the company move forward.

Crisis leadership

The flames in the backyard of the industrial plant where I was a junior engineer were climbing 300 feet in the air. A faulty valve connection on a 100,000-gallon liquid propane tank was allowing propane to escape as a gas. The tank had become a huge propane torch. The primary danger was that as the tank neared empty, the flow of gas would become intermittent, the flame would be sucked back into the tank, and it would explode. This would trigger catastrophic explosions in the five other similar-sized tanks nearby. It could literally destroy the plant, spreading fire and destruction to the nearby town. In this unanticipated calamity, leaders huddled – but no one seemed to have a response.

Suddenly my boss, a senior engineer, stepped forward and said, "If the fire department has an asbestos firefighting suit, I'll put it on, and if you cover me with firefighting foam, I'll go to the valve (where the flames were shooting out) and try to shut it off."

That's what happened. I know because I was there.

That was crisis leadership.

<u>Not exhibiting leadership</u>

A nonprofit organization was sponsoring a roller-skating-themed fund-raiser like a fun run, only with skates. It involved a major effort of obtaining permits, organizing committees and volunteers, obtaining sponsors, marketing…

As the time for the event drew near, it became apparent the event would not meet its goals…in fact, it would be a flop. While staff, board members, and volunteers stayed committed to conducting the event, instead of the disastrous publicity of cancelling it, suddenly the organization's executive director found a need to be out of town on the day of the event. The reason given sounded lame. While the staff and volunteers put a positive face on the event for those who did participate, it was certainly noticed that the leader was not present. It appeared he didn't want to be associated with an event that was not meeting objectives. That ED lost respect and leadership support of staff and board because of this. He had not "walked the talk" of the event…leaving town rather than facing the music.

Resources

Lincoln on Leadership copyright 1992 by Donald T. Phillips II. This is a creative look at Abraham Lincoln's leadership principles, with bullet point summaries.

The Seven Things Your Team Needs to Hear You Say: Lead Productive, Energized, and Innovative Teams Today copyright 2013 by David M. Dye.
The title describes what's in this "to the point" book based on David's personal experience.

Both these books are relatively short, get to the point, and have good end-of-chapter summaries.

Get Started:

1. Make a list of traits you most admire in a leader.

2. Look around and observe people whose leadership you respect and follow, regardless of their position in the organization.

3. Compare what these individuals do with the list at the beginning of this chapter. Add to the list as appropriate.

HOW TO CREATE FUN IN AN ORGANIZATION

The Overview

People who enjoy working for organizations are almost always more effective and productive than those who don't. One way to help people enjoy work is by creating fun in the organization. Fun does not mean telling jokes. Jokes can be a dangerous thing, since they often have inappropriate topics such as politics, gender, and ethnicity as their subjects. Plus, not everyone is skilled in telling jokes. Even comedians struggle to make their jokes work.

Fun is different. It's a positive atmosphere with appropriate humor, along with social and personal interfaces that help build personal, professional relationships, lighten the mood, and make it a positive experience to be and work in the organization.

The Details

The elements of fun are specific to an organization and its culture. Here are some basic principles and ideas to help get you started on creating fun in your organization.

- **Keep score on key metrics in your area and share it with the organization.**

One element of organizational fun is to simply know how the organization is doing relative to its objectives. Giving members of the organization regular progress updates is part of creating the fun. In sports they call this keeping score. Caution: Avoid making this like a "look at me and how well I'm performing" exercise. Keeping score should be a team thing.

Real-World Experience

<u>*How are we doing?*</u>

The new sales manager realized that while there were individual sales goals for salespeople, there was no overall department goal, and no one had any idea how the department was doing on a regular basis. So, she began by simply sending daily emails to everyone in the department, letting them know the department's total sales versus its monthly objective.

Everyone got interested. "How are we doing?" became part of the daily conversation and fun. It motivated employees to perform and to add to the sales tally. Over time this evolved into more sophisticated "score keeping" and small celebrations, including lunch with the sales manager (at her expense, of course) whenever the department exceeded its overall monthly sales goals. An annual team building trip to a local resort was hosted by the sales manager when the total team exceeded its annual goal.

Resource: visit <u>www.openbookmanagement.com</u>

- **Celebrate organization and individual successes…and other things worth celebrating.**

Celebrate successful completion of projects; milestones such as individual and organizational anniversaries; major organizational achievements (such as victories or large sales); public achievements outside the organization by employees; personal celebrations of individuals in the organization, where this seems appropriate for the organization's culture and for the individuals involved (e.g., birthdays, marriages, births, retirements, end of terms, etc.). Celebrations may take the form of simple acknowledgment between individuals; newsletter or email notification to the organization; or more elaborate celebrations, involving food, balloons, plaques, gift cards, or whatever seems appropriate for the level of attainment and the organization's situation.

For more formal celebrations, the organization's leadership is the most appropriate catalyst. For the less formal celebrations, you can take the lead even if you are not the formal leader.

Celebrating "hot"

Occasionally a totally unexpected celebration of something funky can lighten the mood. As president of an industrial distributor with many employees working in a non-air-conditioned shop, on days when temperatures exceeded ninety degrees, I would often walk through our company (including offices) with a big bag of Popsicles, tossing them to employees, letting them know I was "celebrating" the heat. I stopped to chat with employees about their work and challenges. It was funky, fun...and appreciated.

- **Let everyone in the organization know "what's happening" through electronic newsletters, intranets, Facebook, and other internal communication devices.**

This is another way of "keeping score." Keep everyone informed. Keep it fresh. Use people's names in a positive way, and use them a lot.

The newsletter

When I was appointed district sales manager in the Northwest Territory, working with eight distributors from Colorado to Alaska, I established a monthly newsletter for the district, and named it "Moore News in the Northwest." I created a special logo using the two oo's in Moore as eyes, and added my trademark dark-rimmed glasses, as a caricature of ...me.

The newsletter highlighted and celebrated significant sales by individual salespeople and stuff happening outside work that gave positive recognition, and offered sales tips. One salesperson approached me and said, "I know what you're doing. You're getting us excited about seeing our name in the newsletter so we'll want to sell more stuff and get our name in there again. Right?"

Yep.

That's called fun.

- **Create fun events that bring members of the organization together.**

Celebrations and events with food often work very well when it comes to creating a fun, light atmosphere. These might range from something as simple as informal cake and coffee to celebrate a birthday, to the traditional company or organizational picnics or holiday parties. What these interactions really create are opportunities for interpersonal conversations in a lightly structured environment. Conversations build relationships. One guideline: Go heavy on the food, light on the intoxicants.

Real-World Experience

<u>*The chili cook-off*</u>

A frontline employee working for a small company sold the idea of creating an employee chili cook-off. It turns out chili is one of those things that many seem to have an opinion about, and which everyone seems to make a little differently. The event had been scheduled a month in advance, with taste judges appointed, and there were different categories for green and red (and whatever). Prizes and trophies were awarded, and chips and other accouterments were provided. The Master of Ceremonies wore a giant chili pepper hat, and everyone got a taste of all the entries.

It was a success in fostering fun and relationships, and was repeated for several years. One nice feature of the cook-off was that it drew some individuals (as contestants) who were not normally outgoing and social in other environments — but they made a mean chili.

Pancake breakfasts

I discovered a company that would bring all the fixings for a pancake breakfast in and set up within thirty minutes. The griddle looked like a long assembly line for pancakes. As president of the company, I would wear some stupid hat (the Donald Duck hat was a favorite) and do the pancake flipping and serving… occasionally, of course, tossing a pancake at someone. These became quarterly events where employees of different departments could get together for a few minutes to chat, build relationships, make fun of me. Eventually we expanded these pancake breakfasts to include inviting suppliers and customers. Everyone had fun together as the work day started. Fun between employees, suppliers and customers is a good thing.

- **Where the organization is in a facility, create a space where organization members can gather and chat. A break room is one such place.**

  Effective organizations are all about strong personal, professional relationships. A regular place to facilitate informal, interpersonal conversations is part of the fun. If there is no facility for the organization, or no such space in the facility, try a convening at a local coffee shop.

- **Get the organization involved in an outside activity that benefits others.**

Helping and serving others can be a fun team- and relationship-building exercise. Sponsor a blood donation day with a mobile bloodmobile, or an organizational team in a local run benefiting a nonprofit; create a fun United

Way campaign, coordinate a canned food drive, or organize a volunteer work day at a local nonprofit that someone in the organization is involved in – the possibilities are endless. T-shirts and hats with organization logos are inexpensive, appreciated additions. Participation must be on a volunteer basis. If organization members feel coerced into "volunteering," it won't work.

Real-World Experience

<u>Fun run</u>

The nonprofit provided services for children and their families. The clinical staff was primarily comprised of younger people who worked in the homes of those they were serving. As such, they didn't get much chance to get together and build relationships. There was also little opportunity for informal interfaces among the board of directors, administration, and clinical staff.

A local run 5 K run benefitting another nonprofit helping children was announced, and teams were invited from the community. A staff member at the nonprofit (not an identified leader) who liked to run put the word out and a team was formed that included staff, board, and administrators. Members of the board donated team T-shirts with the center logo and registration fees.

They all got together on a Saturday morning, laughed, ran, made fun of each other's abilities, and celebrated some successes. It didn't matter how the team performed; what mattered was the fun and relationships.

<u>Serving dinner</u>

The sales, service, and administrative departments in our company rarely got together. And often normal organizational frictions developed between departments and even individuals from different areas of the company. An employee suggested the company organize volunteers to serve dinner once a month to the homeless at a local center. A list was posted, soliciting volunteers. A mix of individuals from all departments volunteered, including me as president.

The event involved about three hours of serving dinner cooked by the center and helping clean up. There were many opportunities for conversations, making fun of each other, and observing others' values. Personal, professional relationships were developed between individuals of different departments that interfaced but seldom "got together." And, it was fun.

- **Use self-deprecating humor.**

Humor aimed at skewering yourself for some stupid thing you did or some well-recognized trait or habit can be one of the most appreciated ways to create fun in an organization. Most people like to work with people who don't take themselves too seriously and can laugh at themselves. The key here is to not do it so often that it becomes self-degrading; and to make fun of yourself about things that are not critical to your organization function. If you're an electrician, it's not good to make fun of your electrical ability. However, it's okay to make fun of your atrocious spelling on paperwork or your plumbing ability.

Real-World Experience

"Don't hurt yourself, Joe."

Joe worked in an organization that employed many capable technicians, engineers, and IT professionals. Joe's role was sales, sales management, and eventually general management and owner. He was very good at organization, at dealing with people, and at selling. He was terrible at the mechanical and technical aspects of the business.

Rather than be ashamed of this, Joe turned it into his self-deprecating humor. After a while, it became okay for others in the organization to make fun of Joe for his lack of these skills. "Don't give Joe any power tools because he'll hurt himself and others," they would say, or "Joe, I'll replace the battery in your phone so you don't hurt yourself."

None of this reflected on Joe's high-level organizational skills, which were his primary function in the organization. But it did indicate that he didn't take himself too seriously in other areas.

The briefcase

I was promoted to vice president and general manager of the 75-person company I had been with for twelve years. On the way home the evening of the promotion, and armed with new business cards with my vice president title, I was approached in the parking lot by someone who wanted to congratulate me.

At this point I was beginning to feel self-important — a little on the inflated side. After the brief conversation I got in my car and promptly backed over the briefcase that I had set on the ground at the start of the conversation. It, and everything in it, was mangled. I quickly grabbed it, looked around to see if anyone had noticed, shoved it in the car, and left. So much for that "inflated" feeling I was having...

On reflection, I realized this was a wonderful opportunity to use self-deprecating humor. At the next staff meeting, I had the briefcase hidden in a bag. I slowly told the story and then pulled the briefcase out at the punch line moment. There was uproarious laughter. People loved the story and the fact that I could tell it about myself. The kidding was endless: "Gary, when you go home tonight, we'll have some spotters out there when you back up." "Gary, do you have a whole storeroom of briefcases ready just in case?" For years, the briefcase sat in my office to trigger questions from visitors so I could tell the story (exaggerated each time, of course) over and over again. What fun!

- **Gently kid others who can take it...and don't take kidding personally.**

Used appropriately, gentle kidding is a way of making people feel special. It can be a building block for strong personal, professional relationships. Kidding someone can also be dangerous. If you misjudge the person or his or her acceptance level, the kidding can backfire quickly and harm relationships.

The key is to be sensitive to others and willing to accept kidding yourself.

Subjects often safe to kid about include an individual's favorite sports teams; activities outside the organization; personal habits or traits that are pronounced and not negative; or something the person is very good at and which leads to their success (e.g., kidding someone about being very organized, or very assertive, or very good at phone manners).

Real-World Experience

<u>The ice fisherman and the elder statesman</u>

Ken was new in the role of development director for a nonprofit organization. He was paired up with Winston, who was board chair for development. Winston learned early in working together that Ken was both a wonderful community networker and an ice fisherman. After developing the relationship and sensing Ken had a sense of humor and did not take himself too seriously, Winston let Ken know he hated fishing and thought ice fishing was the dumbest form of it. After all, how could sitting outside in the cold waiting for something (probably nothing) to happen be fun or entertaining? He would send Ken cartoons and articles on ice fishing, with comments added to show how dumb Winston thought it was. He gave Winston a stupid fish hat.

Ken loved the kidding and gave it right back to Winston, including sending him a delivery of a frozen fish as a gift. Ken kidded Winston about being a senior citizen and referred to him as the "elder statesman" of the organization." Ken's hair was white and he was not sensitive about it. Ken would often refer to Winston as "my white-haired partner in crime." Winston would fire back that his hair had been dark black before meeting Ken. They formed a close working relationship. Others in the organization caught onto the kidding and joined in. It was fun. More importantly, the organization's fund-raising was very effective, and positively impacted by the personal, professional relationship Ken and Winston developed through mutual kidding about things neither was sensitive about.

- **Here's a weird one…use funny hats or costumes.**

Okay, this won't work for everybody, but it did for me. I had chili pepper hats, duck hats, frog hats, a Superman costume, a gorilla welding mask, a fish hat, a top hat, and a Viking hat with long hair, among others. I used these props in different organizations. They seemed out of character with my normal, buttoned-up persona, and the occasional use of these caught people by surprise, got a laugh, and stuck in people's minds. I've seen this done effectively by others in different organizations. And for some reason, people love to take pictures of others in funny hats and costumes, and even selfies of themselves in stupid hats. It's fun.

Real-World Experience

Superman

When I joined the organization as sales manager, I was looking for a way to break the ice with the close-knit group of salespeople – all of whom were older and more experienced than I was. For a reason no longer clear to me, I got the idea of renting a Superman costume, putting my business suit over it, and in the middle of my first sales meeting – after declaring that I wanted to learn from the group and didn't want to be treated as special – I disrobed and appeared as Superman.

The joke bombed. The room was dead silent. No one got the joke…it wasn't a good joke. After a very uncomfortable moment, I moved on. I tried to forget it. A year and a half later, after I had success moving the organization forward, I was called to the break room. There was an eight-foot-tall rectangular box gift wrapped with my name on it. I unwrapped it to find a phone booth with a Superman costume with my name added to it. I was now Superman Moore. Of course I put it on; now the costume was the joke.

For years afterward, at annual meetings, pancake breakfasts, or other places where employees gathered, I'd disrobe to applause as Superman Moore was revealed. I also used this several times with different groups. I guess it was the juxtaposition of my relatively conservative demeanor, complete surprise, and somewhat self-deprecating nature of the event that got the laughs.

Eventually a picture of Superman Moore appeared on the cover of a national industry publication — further proof that fun, costumes and organizational effectiveness can go hand in hand.

Resource

Do an Internet search on "Fun in the Workplace" and you'll turn up a lot of great ideas on this subject.

Get Started:

1. Identify an obvious shortcoming of yours and use it to create some self-deprecating humor.

2. Create a relationship-building, fun event for the organization.

3. Sell the event to the leaders using the skills outlined in the "How to Sell Your Ideas" chapter of this book.

HOW TO FIND A MENTOR AND HOW TO BE A MENTOR

The Overview

As he left for the Trojan War in *The Odyssey*, Odysseus placed his son Telemachus in the care and guidance of an elder named Mentor. Over centuries, *mentor* came to mean an experienced or trusted advisor; as a verb it also means advising or training someone, especially a younger colleague.

You will benefit by both finding a mentor and mentoring others as you grow in an organization. Mentors can:

- Help you get up to speed quickly
- Describe the informal organization chart
- Fill you in on "how things really work around here"
- Caution you on possible CLMs (career-limiting moves)
- Alert you to opportunities
- Give feedback on your input and initiatives
- Put a good word in for you with people you don't know and in meetings you can't attend (he or she can be your advocate!)

When you *become* a mentor, you provide all of the above for someone else. In return, you get a strong personal, professional relationship with someone you can call on later for support in initiatives or programs you are championing. As trust grows, you will also learn things from the person you are mentoring. It's a great way to get an alternative perspective, which is always important in moving organizations forward. All of this is in addition to the personal satisfaction of being a mentor – helping someone achieve their potential.

As both you and your mentee move onto other organizations, you will commonly give positive referrals for each other and invite each other to join other organizations.

Mentoring is so widely acknowledged today as a means to help build strong relationships in the organization, as well as transmit institutional knowledge, that many organizations have formal mentoring programs (i.e., matching new members of an organization with more experienced ones). There are books written about this process. However, some of the best mentoring in organizations is spontaneous, informal, not structured, without ever using the word *mentor*.

The Details
- **To find a mentor**

When you join an organization, become engaged in the organization's activities immediately by attending meetings, asking relevant questions, and volunteering for appropriate assignments. Make these moves and a mentor will likely find you. You will be noticed and someone will reach out for coffee, or a conversation, or some other connection point. Your primary responsibility is to stay aware and open to the initiative, and responsive to their suggestions.

A more assertive way to find a mentor is to look around the organization for someone you respect and who seems welcoming. Invite that person to coffee or for a conversation. Ask meaningful, open-ended questions about the organization and how it functions. Mention some ways that you feel you can contribute. By reaching out, you are flattering the person and giving the opportunity for a personal, professional relationship to develop.

Unless the organization has a formal mentoring program, it is best not to specifically ask someone if he or she will be your mentor. This approach can be somewhat alienating, and may imply a more formal relationship than the other person is ready for or interested in. An alternate phrase that can be effective to begin a mentoring relationship is, "Jenny, you're pretty experienced with this; can you coach me on the best way to approach this subject with Janice? Or, an alternative way of getting this project approved?"

The best mentoring relationships often develop via this kind of "intentionalization" without formally using the word mentor.

- **To be a mentor**

When you, as a more experienced member of an organization, see a new member quickly becoming engaged, asking questions, volunteering appropriately, and/or making contributions, reach out to that person.

You mentor by example and by specifically offering help to a new member of the organization. "Bill, would you like a little coaching on the best way to work with Tim?" or "Kathy, can I give you a little unsolicited guidance on that project?" The person you reach out to will most likely be flattered, and inspired to "up their game" by contributing more to the organization or living up to your expectations. The mentoring relationship solidifies as that person then reaches out to you with more questions, asking for more information, feedback, and guidance.

There is no need to use the phrase "Let me be your mentor." Just make it happen.

Real-World Experience

<u>The star quarterback reaches out</u>

As this is written, a former professional football player is quoted in the newspaper regarding his time as a rookie on a professional team over nineteen years ago. The article states:

"The star quarterback called him over and told the young receiver that if he had questions, to ask him. 'He said we were going to spend a lot of time together at practice during the season. So it was a vote of confidence that I was going to be on the team at that time when I didn't know nothing from nothing. I will always remember that.'" This professional football player eventually became head coach of a team managed by – yes, you guessed it – his former mentor.

This is the essence of informal, but powerful, mentoring. A spontaneous offer to guide the newer member of the organization. And it is remembered nineteen years later.

<u>*Mentoring appreciated*</u>

Over a thirty-year period, the sales manager had worked with many different salespeople in his company. Five years after leaving the organization, he spontaneously received the following thank-you note from a salesperson he had hired twice in the organization, and worked with (leading, mentoring, managing) for over twenty years:

"Thanks for teaching me to look past selling equipment and see customers' real needs. Thanks for teaching me to find humor in difficult situations. I know I could never have been a leader in other organizations if it had not been for observing how you run a sales organization. Thanks for teaching me the value and benefits of hard work. Thanks for all you modeled for me."

That is the essence of quiet, example mentoring. And the word "mentor" was never used between them.

Get Started

 I. Identify at least one person who has mentored you in an organization or in your personal or career life. Recall how this mentoring was initiated.

2. What did you learn from that mentor?

3. What are your strengths for mentoring another person?

4. Identify someone you'd like to mentor. Reach out.

HOW TO BALANCE YOUR LIFE

The Overview

As your involvements grow and your career advances, you will be subject to increasing time and life pressures. Balancing those pressures becomes a major life skill – one that will be crucial in determining your effectiveness when working in organizations. The pressures you can expect to deal with include:

- Conflicting priorities
- Time crunch
- Financial
- Social
- Personal
- Business
- Career
- Health
- Fitness
- Family
- Relationships
- Personal interests
- Expectations of others
- Peer pressure
- Having fun!

If you do not learn how to manage your life in the face of these and other pressures, you will not only be ineffective in organizations, but you will most likely not meet your personal or professional goals. More importantly, you will not be able to enjoy life to the fullest.

A first step in finding balance in your life is acknowledging that it's important, and that you alone are responsible for it. You can obtain help and advice in dealing with these pressures, but in paraphrasing a recent advertising slogan of the Lincoln Financial Group: "You are your own Chief Life Officer."

The Details

Both in and out of organizations, as individuals are recognized for their skills and their willingness to accept responsibility, they will naturally be asked to join more organizations and accept more responsibilities.

An old expression states, "If you want to get something done, ask someone who's too busy to do it." This indicates that really busy people have already been recognized as skillful in managing their commitments and willing to take on additional responsibilities. The problem is, if you are this sort of person, you can become overloaded and your life can be unbalanced. Tips for balancing your life and managing these pressures include:

- Develop your personal board of advisors (as described in the Bonus section of this book) early. These professionals who know and respect you can be an excellent sounding board as pressures build. This can include people in your life commonly called "mentors."

- Take control of your diet and nutrition.

- Assume responsibility for your health; choose and establish relationships with health-care professionals you trust.

- Begin an exercise regimen in an activity you enjoy enough to maintain over time. Exercise relieves stress and helps put things in perspective. It also provides opportunities for positive social contacts (also known as "friends")!

- Take a time and priority management class and develop a system that works for you. See Skills section of this book for further information and resources.

- Learn how to say "no." Say "no" to joining organizations that don't contribute to your personal or professional objectives. Say "no" when you know you can't effectively take on more responsibilities. Say "no" to destructive social contacts and activities. Say "no" to addictions and other self-destructive behaviors.

- If you find yourself in a downward spiral on any level, get help – from family, professionals, religious counselors, or wherever you need to get it. Don't be afraid to admit you need help.

- Find at least an hour a week (or preferably a few minutes each day) for quiet time, reflection, and meditation. This might be through some formal structure (such as religion or a meditation class), or it might be through the self-discipline of shutting out noise and turning off electronic devices and reflecting on where you are going and how you are getting there.

- Financial pressures can create other types of pressures, so stay out of serious debt and manage your finances conservatively.

- Take vacations.

- Have some fun every day.

- Listen when a friend or associate comments on your overload and lack of balance.

Real-World Experience

<u>Help with a major business and life change</u>

After ten years of owning of a company I had been with for decades, I suddenly realized I was no longer enjoying it, and consequently was not providing the appropriate leadership. I decided to sell the company.

The sales process began to overload me and I began to suffer situational depression. I stayed home several days, after years of never missing work. A member of my personal board of advisors and one of my mentors called me back one day after a lengthy phone conversation and simply stated: "Gary, you are not doing well. You need help to complete this transaction." I listened and got help.

I completed the sales process and moved on to another career. I had allowed myself to lose balance, but had listened when a friend and associate confronted me with this.

Resources

For help with financial pressures, visit
www.daveramsey.com

or

www.suzeorman.com

Plenty of financial management tools are available on both sites. Suze Orman's site also has personal organization and time management tools.

Get Started

1. Ask a friend, partner, or colleague what area of your life seems out of balance to them.

2. Ask them to suggest how you might address this problem.

3. If you haven't already done so, join a health or exercise club; yoga, martial arts, or other class. Get involved with regular physical exercise.

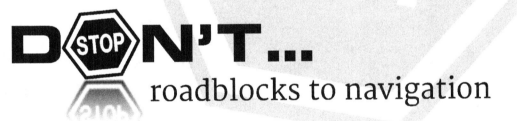

The Overview

Through experience and observation, I have learned of many actions and behaviors in organizations that are counterproductive to being effective…and to the effectiveness of the organizations.

Here are

The Details

Don't…

- **Let social media and personal activities distract you from the work at hand.**

A recent survey of employers in the distribution industry cited on-the-job use of social media for non-organization-related activities as one of their biggest pet peeves. This includes personal texting, managing personal email, personal cell phone conversations, and visiting and posting on Facebook, looking at digital devices for unrelated reasons during meetings and conversations. Yes, generations see this differently. But when someone hires you or asks you to do a job, they generally are positively impressed when you actually do it, instead of mixing significant personal activities with the task at hand.

Don't…

- **Be afraid to ask questions about what's going on and why it's done that way.**

Honest curiosity is a great way to learn about the organization and attract attention as someone who is interested in learning. The best way to get up to speed about what's going on in an organization you have recently joined is to ask open-ended questions that begin with *who, what, why, how, when, and where.*

For example:

What happens to this report when I complete it?

What are the key objectives of this project?

How often does the Executive Committee meet?

How is this budget established?

Who are our biggest customers?

What are the major issues we face?

Why are the committees organized this way?

What's the organization chart look like?

Who are the folks who really move the organization forward?

Why do we do this? Why do we do it this way? Have we ever considered a different approach?

These questions should be asked in a non-accusatory way. These should be honest questions about what is going on so you can learn and contribute more quickly.

Real-World Experience

<u>*Questions asked, questions not asked…*</u>

Bill was appointed to a three-year term on his church's Finance Committee. On the balance sheet of the organization was a list of restricted funds that no one discussed or asked questions about. Finally, after several meetings, Bill asked: "Who has responsibility for these funds? How do we decide when to spend them?" There was silence; no one knew. Bill asked for and was given responsibility for the funds, and over the next year he investigated each of them and helped the church spend them to accomplish its mission within original donor restrictions. Bill continued to ask probing questions after becoming chairperson of the committee.

In a related area, Bill thought it was strange that the church administrator didn't have working hours that matched business hours. He also seemed to be a bad communicator, not always answering emails promptly, and sometimes alienating church members in his abrupt response to their questions. At the end of one year, the church auditor identified irregularities with the administrator, and he was dismissed. Bill later found others had also felt things in this area were not quite right, but no one had asked why things were done this way.

Get Started

1. What is going on in your organization that you don't quite understand or would like to know more about?

2. Who can you approach about these questions?

3. How will you structure the questions?

Don't...

- **Take stuff personally (but assume everyone else does).**

We all tend to take things personally. We don't get a promotion or position we hoped for; we overhear a negative comment; our ideas are rejected; we don't connect with someone we reached out to; we don't get invited to a meeting or social event; we aren't copied on an email we learn about later; or, we simply get a "look" we interpret as negative. Often we take these as intended personal slights or rejection. Our judgment becomes clouded with emotions such as hurt, anger, lack of self-confidence, and, in the extreme, a desire to "get back" at someone or at the organization. Ouch! That sort of thinking will not make you effective in any organization.

Instead, these issues should be seen as routine, organizational hurdles to overcome. In many cases they are unintended or even "made up" in our own minds. The proper response is often no response. Or, use your self-confidence to ignore the personal aspect and move forward with whatever your next steps are for the organization.

We should also assume that everyone else <u>will</u> take perceived slights or rejection personally. It's a human reaction that, while avoiding it ourselves, we should anticipate in others. This will lead you to broaden your contacts and relationships; include more people in your communications and invitations to meetings; empathize with others; avoid sarcastic or personal comments or judgments; and be alert to situations where people might take things personally, thereby affecting their demeanor or actions.

Another way of expressing this is an excerpt from Rudyard Kipling's poem "If":

"If you can keep your head when all about you / Are losing theirs and blaming it on you…"

I encourage you to find a copy of the complete text of this poem and read it. Much of it is good advice for being effective in organizations – and in life.

Real-World Experience

<u>*Taking it personally*</u>

After a nationwide search, the board selected Carolyn to head a small organization. She immediately began to introduce much-needed technology and institute financial controls. This was a cultural change for the organization, and as is common in similar situations, she encountered objections and roadblocks.

Carolyn was working through these issues when she began to take criticism of her methods personally. She couldn't let this go and began to focus her sense of persecution on one of the organization's key people – the Human Relations (HR) manager. Then, she began to suspect that anyone she saw conversing with the HR manager was criticizing her, and she started the process of firing the HR manager. This came to the attention of the board of director's Executive Committee, who saw things differently and began to examine how this was negatively impacting the organization. Ultimately Carolyn was dismissed, and the HR manager survived.

Get Started:

1. The next time you feel you have suffered a personal slight in the organization, forget about it and move on.

2. When you next hear a piece of gossip about someone in the organization, forget it and don't pass it on.

Don't...

- **Spend significant time around negative people.**

Reverend Dr. Norman Vincent Peale was an American preacher, author, and self-help guru in the middle 20th century, whose most famous book was *The Power of Positive Thinking*. First published in 1952, it described the importance of thinking positively in helping individuals reach their goals. There is also a "Power of Negative Thinking." Unfortunately, that power drags people and organizations down. In many organizations there are one or more persons who are dissatisfied, disgruntled, or disappointed in their situation. They make this known by complaining, grumbling, and in some cases working against the goals of the organization, and even against their own welfare and goals! I call them Dr. No.

Like flypaper, these people often attract others who can be swayed or who might be moderately dissatisfied. And, like flypaper, once attracted to this negativity, it's difficult to break free. If you get drawn into this circle, you, too, may become dissatisfied. At best you may have your positive energy reduced; at worst, you may divert your energy in counterproductive directions. It will become known that you are a part of the "negative gang." That will almost immediately reduce your effectiveness and negatively impact your progress in the organization. One way to deal with negative people is to simply avoid them. You don't have to preach positivism to them, but stay away from them as much as you can.

Real-World Experience

<u>New sales manager and Dr. No</u>

The new manager from "outside" was introduced to a close-knit organization that formerly had worked directly for the owners of the medium-sized company. As the manager began to make changes, one of the employees in his area of responsibility, Larry, decided to try to push him out of the organization. He began an "around the water cooler" (actually, over lunch, during bowling league games, and at after-work social hours) negative campaign.

"The new manager doesn't understand what we have to deal with; is too tough; is making the wrong changes; is never going to last; is not one of us." Larry was Dr. No. Some members of the organization bought into this, but most didn't. The manager, while aware of this, simply ignored it. He went about the business of moving the organization forward. Within eighteen months most of the negative gang, including Dr. No, were gone. Some quit and others were dismissed.

Get Started:

1. Identify the negative people in your organization.

2. Avoid these people.

Don't…

- **Spend significant personal time with supervisors and employees who are working for you.**

It seems like a natural thing to do to build relationships: spend personal time with employees who work for you or with you, or, better yet, with your boss. The problem is that significant personal time – outside of work – spent with employees who work for you creates the following challenges:

- Tendencies to make allowances for work that doesn't meet expectations. "He's a good guy so I'll let that go for now."

- Awkwardness when decisions need to be made. For example, telling a friend that they aren't meeting expectations is a lot tougher than telling that to someone you have a personal but essentially professional relationship with.

- Potential rivalries when spending time with some employees but not with others.

- Situations where things happening on personal time negatively impact work situations.

- Atmospheres where gossip, being negative, or complaining become predominant topics of conversation.

When spending significant time with your supervisor, the same issues develop for them and for you in reverse. Offhand comments or comments made in jest can be taken and remembered in the wrong context. And these situations can definitely create jealousy within an organization, with suggestions made that decisions are based on personal relationships, not the merits of situations. That is not good for any organization.

Of course, in most organizations there will be downtime spent with supervisors and other employees. It is best to keep this downtime relatively structured, focusing on mostly organization-sponsored activities held without any specific frequency.

Real-World Experience

Breaking the cycle

The owner of a small company had developed the habit of meeting some employees each day after work at a local restaurant, where they told stories, discussed sports teams, and generally socialized. Gradually, the owner found that his business decisions were becoming more difficult because of the relationships developed at the restaurant. After all, it's hard to tell your buddies that they are not cutting it, or institute unpopular but needed policy changes. He also learned employees who did not join the group resented these meetings. They assumed stories being told involved employees not attending these after-work sessions. They began to take it personally.

To break this cycle, the owner hired an outside chief executive officer (CEO) to report to him; all other employees were under the responsibility of the new CEO. The latter never joined the after-work group, didn't participate in the various employee social groups, and spent very little personal time with the owner. Soon, the after-work sessions disappeared.

The CEO did participate in structured company social activities like the softball team, company picnics, company golf tournament, and United Way fund-raising campaigns (which he turned into fun, relationship-building events). He created formal relationship/team building events using professional facilitators.

While developing personal, professional relationships throughout the organization, the CEO never developed strictly personal relationships or friendships with some employees to the exclusion of others. The company grew and was seen as a leading professional organization.

Don't...

- **Ignore anyone in the organization.**

Some people in organizations are ignored. These can include administrative support employees, behind-the-scenes IT workers, and security and custodial employees. Yet, these individuals can be key to the effective everyday workings of most organizations. Personal, professional relationships can be just as important here as with more prominent members of the organization.

When interfacing with these employees, be sure to initiate contact and communication. When interfacing in person, look them in the eye and offer to shake their hands. "Hi, I'm Gary Moore, new with the organization." Many will respond with their names, but some may not due to lack of confidence. If they don't, be sure to ask their name and then follow up with "What's your area of responsibility here?" "How long have you been with the organization?" and "What can I do to make your job easier?" Thank them for their help. You never know when you will need it.

Real-World Experience

<u>*Speedy*</u>

As graduate dorm counselor at a large state university, I was responsible for the undergraduates and facilities of my floor. Early on I sought out the custodian. He was caught somewhat off guard by my attention. None of the other counselors had bothered. I asked his name. He grinned and said, "They just call me Speedy."

I quickly learned that he had a nervous condition and did everything at triple speed. At times, this appeared awkward, and subjected him to some ridicule. But I soon observed Speedy got the job done...and quickly! I asked Speedy his biggest problem on my floor and he told me that it was a couple of very messy, inconsiderate undergraduates. I addressed the situation and he appreciated it. He gave my floor extra attention. He often sought me out to tell me about things I needed to know.

Once, Speedy warned me about a student who was considering jumping from a window. Without this relationship, built on mutual respect and trust, I may not have gotten the situation handled in time. It's been over 45 years and I don't know if Speedy remembers me, but I certainly remember him, our personal, professional relationship, and the important work he did for the school.

<u>The A-V and room setup guys</u>

In my "third career" as a seminar leader, speaker, and trainer, I often walk into meeting rooms an hour or so before attendees begin to arrive. I immediately seek out the audiovisual specialists, who are responsible for projection and sound, and the room setup supervisors. I introduce myself, ask their names, shake their hands, and thank them for their work. I give them some context, including where I come from, the purpose of the meeting, and the organization that is sponsoring it.

I then ask them to make the modifications I need to customize the room for my purposes. In spite of requirements being emailed ahead of time, some changes are almost always needed once I actually see the room. I always get better cooperation by establishing these brief personal, professional relationships than if I were to just walk in and complain (which is the style of some of my colleagues).

Don't...

- **Take your complaints outside of the organization.**

Some members of organizations like to complain about the organization, its leadership, its members, procedures, policies, and many other things. Legitimate complaints, examined openly and dealt with professionally within the organization, can be constructive tools for improvement. However, taking complaints outside of the organization is detrimental to the organization. It can also make you look silly for continuing to work for an organization you are complaining about.

In today's world, complaining often takes the form of "digital gossip," or posts on Facebook, tweets, You Tube videos, and sarcastic emails. As we have all come to learn, digital communication isn't private and it can seldom be totally erased.

When you have legitimate, minor complaints in an organization, it's up to you to help fix the problem. When you have major complaints, work to bring these to the attention of persons you respect in positions of authority, along with any recommendations you have to improve the situation. It makes sense to follow the chain of command with this process. When offering suggestions for change, use some of the techniques discussed in the "How to Sell Your Ideas" chapter.

If major complaints are not dealt with, and if you feel these are detrimental to your progress in the organization or to the organization itself, consider leaving the organization.

Exception:

If you are aware of a situation that might violate significant legal, ethical, or safety standards and you've brought this to the attention of appropriate people in the organization but nothing has been done about it...try again. If at all possible, it is in your and the organization's best interests to resolve these sorts of issues from within. In many cases, you may find you don't have all the facts or that it simply needed to be brought to the attention of the right people. Many organizations appreciate these situations being brought to the attention of the right people so they can be corrected.

If the situation is not corrected in this manner, you have two choices:

- *leave the organization or*
- *consider being a whistle-blower.*

"Whistle-blower" is a term used for someone who takes a major complaint to some authority outside the organization, or who otherwise publicizes the situation outside the organization. This should be a last resort and you must be confident

that you are right and that the issue is important enough for this type of external exposure / accusation. Be aware of potential consequences of whistle-blowing, including losing your job or place in the organization; being subjected to public criticism or even persecution. Whistle-blowers are often shunned for employment in future situations. However, in a few cases, usually involving significant safety, moral, ethical, or legal issues, the exposure of a situation is worth that risk.

Don't...

- ## Do stupid stuff on social media.

Some people seem to think that the virtual world of social media is or should be outside the realm of their "real world" of work or organizations. That is a serious mistake. Your digital footprint quickly becomes part of your record and image. What you say or do in these realms has real consequences and is almost sure to be noticed by someone who will relate it back to you. Inappropriate pictures, statements, posts, and tweets all reflect on you and the organization that you are a part of, and they almost never go away.

Real-World Experience

<u>Ill-considered tweets</u>

A retired, prominent professional ballplayer had a following on Twitter. He used this platform to make a congratulatory tweet about his daughter and her achievements as a pitcher on her university softball team. A number of people who did not know the baseball player or his daughter, apparently thinking they were either anonymous or that they were just "tweeting" so it didn't matter, tweeted derogatory, vulgar comments about the ballplayer's daughter. Her father decided to act and tracked down these individuals. He mounted a campaign against them. At least two lost their jobs and some may be sued. Remember: the virtual world is the real world.

Don't...

- **Work for an extended period of time for someone you don't respect.**

When you work with or for someone, it is important that you respect him or her. You do not need to always agree with, like, or be friends with your boss, but you should respect that person. If you don't, it could be time to look for a different position in the organization, or even to leave. Of course, when you don't respect your boss, you may not always be in a position to immediately change jobs or supervisors. However, you should look for every opportunity to make a change as early as possible. In the meantime, try to put your head down and do your job.

Real-World Experience

<u>*New boss — not a good match for me*</u>

I had been with a major corporation for four years, growing in responsibility and pay each year. I worked sequentially for managers with different styles and expectations, but I trusted and respected them, and they gave sound advice.

Then I was promoted to a regional manager's position, working for a person I found insincere. He often made promises to customers that he failed to keep, and told me to "just deal with it." Finding my progress in the company blocked by this manager whom I did not respect professionally, I sought employment outside of the corporation. I found a job with an industry leader, accepting it with a drop in pay, but working for owners and partners I instantly respected. The new situation seemed to offer future opportunity. I stayed for three decades, building a successful career and eventually owning the company.

Don't...

- **Complain about the organization after you leave.**

When you leave an organization of your own volition, are laid off, or have your employment terminated (fired!), just move on. There is no future in complaining. They are part of your past – not your future. When you complain about a former employer, a prospective employer is always thinking, "I wonder what the other side of that story is? I wonder if this person will start complaining about us if we hire them and if they ever leave us?" This will most likely lead them to be wary of hiring you.

If you leave a job for negative reasons, one reply to the interview question "Why did you leave your previous employer?" is some form of "We had different views of expectations in my position, and it seemed best to move on." Or simply "It just wasn't a good fit." When follow-up questions are asked, be honest but positive (or at least neutral) about your previous employer.

Perhaps just as importantly, when you begin complaining about a former employer, you become "Dr. No." Your mind-set is negative and it is more difficult for you to focus on your future in a positive manner.

Real-World Experience

<u>*"I didn't start the fight."*</u>

As a manager and later the owner of a midsized firm, over a several decade time span I reviewed thousands of resumes and interviewed hundreds of people for potential employment. I often reviewed resumes and cover letters where significant space was allocated to complaining about previous employers. Perhaps the most interesting paragraph I found on a resume was one describing how the fistfight at his previous employer was not the applicant's fault, followed by excruciating detail of how the "other employee" started the fight. Really? Describe this in a resume?

I seldom chose to interview people who complained about their previous employer in their cover letters and resumes. And, I never hired a person who spent significant interview time complaining about their previous employer.

Don't...

- **Violate legal, ethical, or moral boundaries.**

Governments, as a reflection of their constituencies, set *legal boundaries.* Organizations such as companies, trade associations, and professional societies set *ethical standards*, both written and implied. Ultimately, we each set our own *moral boundaries*, guided by parents, society, the groups we are part of, and in some cases, religion.

Actions that are legal may not be ethical or moral. Actions that are ethical may not meet our individual moral standards. Actions have consequences. As we choose to violate any of these standards relating to the organizations that we belong to, we put those organizations at risk. More importantly, perhaps, we put ourselves at risk.

If you are in doubt about any of these boundaries relative to an organization, you have an obligation to stop, get the appropriate guidance, and make decisions not to violate the boundaries. Guidance for each set of boundaries may vary. Legal guidance can come from the organization's senior management or respected attorneys – possibly those associated with the organization or perhaps a personal attorney. Guidance for ethical issues may require consulting professionals more experienced in that area, trade associations, or written ethical guidelines.

Regarding moral boundaries, you should first consult yourself and your conscience, and then talk to other respected advisors in those areas. These boundaries may not always be specifically defined; there are "gray" areas of uncertainty. If you feel boundaries are about to be crossed, you have an obligation to discuss these concerns with your organization's leadership. In the extreme, if you're being asked or forced to violate these boundaries, you may need to resign. It's that important.

- See also the "Exception" under the **Don't take your complaints outside of the organization** chapter of this section.

Real-World Experience

"What's in it for me?"

Ron, the long-term, professional engineer in charge of purchasing major equipment for the nationwide manufacturing company, had an outstanding reputation in his company and industry. He was a technology leader who published several articles about "best practices" in industry publications.

Glen, the sales manager for a firm selling equipment to Ron, had an excellent personal, professional relationship with him. Glen sold Ron a lot of equipment that worked well for Ron's company. It was a mutually beneficial relationship.

Then, tragically, Ron died of a rapidly advancing illness. He was replaced by Ben. Glen noticed in the first orders from Ben that Ben made mistakes and expected Glen's company to absorb the cost of those errors.

Then, in a sales call regarding a major potential order, Ben not so subtly asked, "What's in it for me if I buy your equipment?" The tone and manner of the question alerted Glen to Ben's apparent unethical expectation. Glen responded with "Well, your company gets some great equipment at a fair price and my personal customer service follow-up." Ben again asked, with emphasis, "I mean, what's in it for <u>me</u>?" Glen did not directly respond, essentially ignoring the question.

Soon Ben was purchasing his equipment elsewhere. While this was a significant blow to both his company's sales and his income, Glen decided that was okay, given Ben's ethical standards and the extra costs Glen was expected to absorb due to Ben's mistakes.

Over time, Ben's company discovered these issues, fired Ben, and barred Glen's competitors who had been successfully selling to Ben from doing further business with the company. Apparently these competitors had indeed found something in the transactions for Ben. Glen and his company were invited to again do business with the company.

SKILLS
for navigating

The Overview

There are several personal and professional skills that can impact your effectiveness and development within an organization and, by extension, the progress of the organization itself.

Some of these skills may seem natural, like listening. However, at a professional and effective organizational level, many of these skills are <u>not</u> natural for many people. Other skills, such as public speaking and making presentations to groups, may be scary to some.

You may already have a high level of proficiency in one of these areas. Leverage that while working to develop others to your potential.

The Details

Important skills for effectiveness in navigating organizations include

- **Using all forms of communication.**

In some technical settings, communication is looked upon as a soft skill. However, in the organizational realm, effective communication may be the single most critical skill to moving the organization forward – and to progressing in an organization.

Quoting George Bernard Shaw (brainyquotes.com):

"The single biggest problem in communication is the illusion it has taken place."

When, in an organizational context, someone says, "They didn't listen to me. They didn't get it. They ignore my ideas," it often means the person doesn't understand that when trying to get a message across to someone, or a group, you will be most effective when you assume:

"You have 100 percent communication responsibility for the target audience to receive and understand your message."

The first rule of effective communication is to *consider the audience*.

Questions to consider when communicating within an organization include:

- Who are you communicating with?
- What is their current level of knowledge on this subject?
- What do they need to know?
- What is their level of interest in the subject being communicated?
- How can you get their attention?
- How do they most effectively receive messages? Written? Oral? Paper? Email? Text? On a mobile device? Via social media? In a casual conversation? In a formal presentation? In person or via phone? How do they react to voice mail? Do they read their emails? Do they listen to voice mail?
- When is the most receptive time for your audience to receive your message? What is the best time of day? days of the week? time of month or year? timing in advance of an event or desired response? What is the most effective time to communicate with whatever else is going on in the audience's lives and schedules? What is their receptivity to hearing this message at this time?

A key element of effective communication is getting the message to your target audience by a means and within a timeframe that ensures they receive and understand it as intended.

- Special note about "communicating up":

There are special considerations about communicating up to your boss, to the organization's leader, to the board, or whomever you may be reporting to. To be effective in this situation, you should always:

- Ask or determine what they want to know, how often, and in what format.

- Test this with your own judgment after you work with them for a while.

- If you are about to make a major decision affecting the organization – and particularly if it involves major money, risk, or people, even if it's clearly in your purview of authority – consider letting your supervisor know the issues and your decision or recommendation ahead of time. You might benefit from their input. You are giving them a heads-up as this major action takes place with the goal of avoiding surprises…particularly negative surprises.

- Consider giving *interim communication* about project status and any major problems. "Our deadline for this project is two months away, but to give you an update on our progress…" They'll appreciate this, even if they don't ask for it.

- Alert leaders or supervisors to pending issues that might be negatively consequential to the organization or that could put the organization at risk. It's better to report this early, along with your current plan of action, than to report bad news as a surprise later. No one likes major negative surprises, and people will often "blame the messenger."

- Delight leaders with some good news occasionally, but not so often as to appear self-aggrandizing. Give them good news, and where appropriate, give someone who works for (or with) you the credit!

The next six skills in this chapter deal with specific communication skills important for organizations.

Resources

Search online for "training communication skills for organizations" and you will find many sources.

Get Started

1. What are your communication strengths? How do you leverage these?

2. What are your communication weaknesses? How can you work to strengthen them?

3. Identify how you like to receive communication: Oral? Written? Formal? Informal? Social media? Then consider how this might be different with others you communicate with.

- **Asking Open-Ended Questions**

Open-ended questions cannot be answered with a simple yes or no. They encourage and require the responder to talk, elaborate, and provide meaningful answers.

Open-ended questions begin with the words *who, what, why, how, when,* or *where.* Here are a few examples:

What are your objectives for this project?

Who can help us achieve these goals?

What are the biggest challenges the organization faces?

Why is the committee organized that way?

When is the deadline for getting this done?

Open-ended questions avoid the assumptions often contained in closed-ended questions, such as:

Is growth your biggest challenge?
(assumes growth is an issue, implies it's the biggest challenge)

Your objectives seem to be growth and better customer service…is that true?
(assumes growth and customer service are organization objectives)

It takes discipline to consistently use open-ended questions, but they are the beginning of learning and building personal, professional relationships.

Rudyard Kipling said (www.kiplingsociety.co.uk. from *The Elephant's Child*):

"I keep six honest serving men; (they taught me all I knew);
Their names are what and why and when
And how and where and who"

The most important next step after asking an open-ended question is often the most difficult part. *Shut up and listen to the answer.*

Advanced question-asking involves asking open-ended questions, actively listening to the answers, and then, instead of responding directly, asking an appropriate follow-up open-ended question! The more the other person talks, the more you will learn about them and their perspective on the organization and other key points. The more the other person talks and the more you listen, the less likely you are to say something counterproductive. After initial opening social amenities, it's always good to ask an open-ended question to get the other person talking first. You gain insights into their perspective on the topic of conversation and can respond in an appropriate manner.

- **Active Listening**

Active listening is a well-recognized skill for negotiations, resolving conflict, and building personal, professional relationships in organizations. Among other things, active listening involves careful listening to the speaker, then feeding the information back in your own words in summary form to ensure understanding.

As I understand it, you are asking for…

In another sense used here, active listening also involves paying attention to the speaker's tone, observing body language, and listening for what has <u>not</u>

been said. Who in the meeting is turning negative on the idea? Why is that person no longer contributing to the discussion?

In organizations, many things are hinted at or happening behind the scenes. The goal of active listening is to understand what is being said, the meaning of what is being said, and – as much as possible – what is not being <u>explicitly</u> said (but that is going on and needs to be understood).

Resources

There are many resources for learning about active listening. Search "active listening" online to find many choices.

- ### Public Speaking; Making Effective Presentations

Many people have a fear of speaking in front of groups of almost any size. If this is you, you will benefit from conquering this fear because public speaking is one of the most effective ways to disseminate information, marshal resources, and sell ideas within an organization. It is also one of the primary ways individuals get noticed in organizations – both favorably and unfavorably. Public speaking is also closely tied to effective meeting management – a skill discussed in the **How to...** section of this book.

Not everyone will become a speaker in the sense of speaking on a stage in front of hundreds of people. But most individuals, and certainly most leaders, within organizations will be called on to speak in front of groups of some size, chair meetings, or make presentations. Doing this well gets you and your ideas noticed. Avoiding it or doing it poorly can hamper progress for both you and for your ideas.

Resources

Most universities and colleges have courses in public speaking. Such programs/classes are also available commercially. However, one of the best resources is the nonprofit organization **Toastmasters International**. This ninety-year-old organization has over 14,000 clubs in 126 countries worldwide. The clubs usually meet weekly. A Toastmasters club provides a safe, structured environment to learn and practice speaking before groups, and provides regular, constructive feedback. And no matter what your level of speaking experience, you only really grow in skill by speaking before groups.

Real-World Experience

Speaking up

I was invited to join the board of a national industry trade association. Relative to the industry, my company was fairly small. When it was suggested at a board meeting that a sales seminar was needed, I immediately volunteered to organize and be the primary speaker at the seminar. Speaking is one of my skills. The seminar was well received and a success.

II became known as a leading speaker in the industry. On the basis of this work, I became president of the board for the association, which led to many productive relationships nationwide. Among them was a contact that ultimately purchased the company I owned.

Building confidence

Glenda was a high-ranking executive, new with her company. At a national meeting, she was asked to introduce a speaker to a large audience. Lacking speaking experience and confidence, she was not pleased with her performance. She knew she could and should do better. A mentor suggested she join a Toastmasters club so she could develop skills and – just as important – confidence in speaking in front of groups.

Glenda took her mentor's advice, joined a local Toastmasters club, and became a confident and skilled speaker. As an industry leader she was invited to speak in many different situations. It became one of her strengths as a leader. Her career, and that of the organization she represented, advanced.

Get Started

1. Visit www.toastmasters.org.

2. Find clubs near you that meet at times convenient for you.

3. Visit at least three clubs as an observing (and, if you want, participating) guest.

4. Join one for at least a six-month trial.

- **Writing**

With in-person meetings and interfaces becoming less and less frequent, communicating effectively in writing is becoming a more valuable skill. Communicating in writing may mean via electronic document, the body of an email, a text, or, in some organizations, on paper.

Good keyboarding skills makes this easier, but with audio software and other means, most anyone can manage effective written communication.

Getting to the point is the key to effective organizational writing. Direct, succinct, straightforward writing gets the message across quickly and without losing the audience's interest. And in today's connected society, it is important to avoid saying anything in writing (electronic or otherwise) that you or the organization may regret later.

Another important writing skill in effective organizations is the ability to summarize quickly (as in an Executive Summary).

The person who can create effective written documents ... personal letters or emails, reports, memos, executive summaries, proposals, recommendations, agendas, meeting minutes or summaries, presentations...can frame the discussions and guide actions in the direction they think appropriate for the organization.

Real-World Experience

One-page position papers

It was said President Ronald Reagan asked for all position papers for his review be a maximum of one page in length. It's unclear if this really happened, but it gets the idea across of getting to the point quickly and succinctly in organizational communication.

• Negotiating

Negotiating is an everyday activity in life and in organizations. Sometimes negotiating involves money. More often it involves negotiating ideas, time, location, procedures, team members, strategic plans, schedules... At some point almost everything is negotiated. These negotiations may take place between individuals or groups within an organization, or among the organization (or someone representing it) and individuals or organizations outside your organization.

Effective negotiation within an organization is critical to avoid harmful disagreements. The best negotiation within an organization is a win-win-win; wins for each individual or group and for the organization as a whole. Almost no one is a "born negotiator," and almost anyone can learn to be an effective one. It is a skill that you will want to learn, develop, and hone over time.

Resources

Search online for "negotiating" or "negotiation," and you'll find a multitude of commercial and academic possibilities. In my experience, a good resource for learning negotiation skills is *Karrass Effective Negotiating.* You can check out their many offerings at <u>www.karrass.com</u>. As Dr. Chester L. Karrass, its founder, stated

"In business, as in life, you don't get what you deserve...you get what you negotiate."

Get Started

1. Visit the website www.karrass.com.

2. Register for their free monthly negotiating tips; you'll automatically get their first ten tips.

- **Conflict Resolution**

Organizations are populated with people, and even people of goodwill disagree – it's a virtual guarantee. They will disagree about money, use of resources, objectives, parking spots, workspace temperature... You name it, they'll disagree about it.

In most healthy organizations these disagreements won't elevate to the level of "conflicts." Instead, they will be resolved fairly easily, perhaps with the help of others in the organization who aren't directly involved in the dispute (i.e., third parties).

However, some disagreements will escalate to a more intense level without being easily resolved by the individuals involved. This is where conflict resolution skills come into play.

Real-World Experience

<u>Professionals conflict</u>

Larry was a top salesperson and Kathy was an experienced executive secretary. Kathy was Larry's primary support person. Both excelled at their jobs and each got along with most other coworkers. But they simply didn't get along with each other.

George, the supervisor, could never quite determine the source of the disagreement. Most likely it was simply personal dislike of the other's style. The personal disagreement began to escalate and become damaging to each person's work and general organization morale. George met with Larry and Kathy individually, asking them to be specific about their issues with the other person. The list was simply not helpful. "I don't like the way he asks me to do projects" Kathy would state. Larry would respond, "I don't like the way she gives me unasked-for feedback on my work. That's not her job." The list went on…

George then met with them together and gave each person the other's feedback. He asked for constructive ideas to reduce the conflict; nothing worked.

Finally, George sent a joint email to the two of them. It said:

"Larry, Kathy:

You are both professionals. I value each of you for the outstanding work you do. You obviously don't get along and I have failed to reduce the tensions. Therefore, I am asking each of you to override personal feelings; minimize your contact with the other while continuing to do your work. Bring me any substantive complaints directly and I will immediately resolve the situation. Otherwise, just do the job and move on. You don't have to be friends, but you do have to respect each other and work together professionally. If either of you do not believe you can do this, let's get together to consider the possibility this is no longer the right place for you to work. Thank you to two professionals from someone who values your work but who will no longer tolerate petty disagreements standing in the way of moving forward.

Thanks, George."

Both stayed with the company, and while they never developed a close personal, professional relationship, they did manage to interface without further major issues. Neither brought any further disagreements to George.

Resources

Managing Conflict in Organizations
by M. Afzalur Rahim, copyright 2001

Conflict Resolution at Work for Dummies
by Vivian Scott, copyright 2010

Get Started

1. In the organizations that you join, note any subjects of conflict you observe.

2. Mentally outline how you, as a leader, might work to resolve the conflict.

- **Time and Priority Management**

Everyone working in the realm of organizations needs to develop their own personal system for time and priority management. It's important to note that time management is keeping track of appointments and tasks, while priority management is the ability – and self-control – to prioritize activities and relationships, and focus on the most urgent, important stuff first. And as *urgent* and *important* don't always coincide, decisions must be made as to which to address first.

These skills are important both in life and within organizations. Implementing these skills requires appropriate time and priority management tools, but don't be fooled. Time and priority management is about more than tools and common calendaring. It is about a mind-set for personal productivity to reach whatever your goals are – both in and out of organizations.

There are references to books and commercial programs and systems to help with this in the following Resources paragraph. However, each individual must develop his or her own customized system.

Resources

The Seven Habits of Highly Effective People
by Stephen Covey, first published in 1989

Check out the programs at www.franklincovey.com, where you can [...]
array of seminars, books, and other tools for time and priority man[...]

Visit www.daytimer.com to review a range of time and priority manage[...]
tools.

Real-World Experience

Getting the team on the same time management page

As a new sales manager, I was striving to be more productive and to help the sales force be more productive. I discovered there was no common personal organization/ time management system and so I created my own, but I found it difficult to "graft" it onto the team.

Then I researched and selected a professional time and priority management system offered by a reputable firm. It included workshops along with electronic and paper tools. I joined all our salespeople and other managers in participating in the seminar at company expense. I offered to pay for all the time management tools the salespeople used. I immediately immersed all new hires in this system through seminars and tools. This gave our sales team a common view of productivity, a common language for discussing productivity, and some common tools. Productivity and sales significantly increased.

Get Started

1. Make a list of your top three time priority conflicts.

2. Make a list of your top three "time wasters."

3. Investigate the cost and availability of at least one time/priority management system.

' Statements

'any informal) organizations have some sort
‿‿, and financial statements that are used to
‿ches, clubs, nonprofits, closely held companies,
‿niversities, one-person companies, entrepreneurial
‿ajor public corporations…the list goes on. If there's more
‿oney involved in the form of dues, contributions, sales revenue,
‿nt capital, expenses, or taxes, there is (or should be) some form
‿nancial reporting involved. In many cases, formal financial reporting to
federal and state governments or agencies is involved.

To be effective in organizations, you need to be aware of what financial statements are produced. Ask for copies of these statements; review them; understand their implications; and then ask questions about what you see and learn.

Examination of financial statements can reveal the financial health of an organization, as well as the problems, opportunities, priorities, sources of power, mistakes, effective use of funds or not, ethical values, and honesty (or, in some cases, dishonesty). It can help you decide whether this is actually an organization you want to continue working with or not.

Key financial statements used by most formal organizations include:

- **Profit / Loss Statement** (sometimes called Income Statement, or P&L or Revenue/Expense Statement) reveals just what it says it does: How is the organization creating revenue, how much is being created, and how is it balancing expenses against this? Where is the money being spent? Over time, this indicates the financial viability of the organization.

- **Cash Flow Statement** indicates the short-term health of the organization. Is the cash going to be there to pay the bills this month? next month? longer term?

- **Budget** and performance against budget indicate priorities and how they are being managed.

- **Balance Sheet** delineates assets such as cash, accounts receivable, and capital equipment; liabilities such as debt; and basic investment in the organization.

You don't have to be a financial professional to review these statements. You should, however, have some familiarity with them and be able to quickly discern trends by comparing several reporting periods.

Caution: You are taking a significant time and money risk by working with any organization that deals with money but does not share accurate, regular financial reporting with its members and stakeholders.

Also, most formal organizations have some required reporting to government entities — even if it's only tax reporting. Public corporations and nonprofit organizations have very specific reporting requirements. These are another source of financial information about the organizations, and they also create legal duties to report for their officers and boards.

Resources

If you're in school now, regardless of your major, consider taking a course in how to read financial statements.

A quick overview can be found in the book-
Reading Financial Reports for Dummies
by Lita Epstein, December 30, 2013

A somewhat more detailed look at this topic can be found in the book
Finance for the Non-Financial Manager
by Gene Siciliano, copyright 2003

Get Started

1. Obtain and review your organization's financial statements.

2. Write down three questions about something you don't understand, or jot down something about the organization's financial condition that concerns you.

3. Seek out the person who prepares these documents and ask him or her your questions.

personal board of
ADVIS👥**RS**
your
navigation
team

The Overview

No one can be a specialist in all areas where you may need professional advice. Yet, most of you will need specialized professional advice as your careers advance, and as your income, assets, and professional and personal responsibilities increase.

Such specialized advice is more customized and helpful if you have a personal, professional relationship with the person who is providing the advice. It is difficult to develop these relationships on short notice. So, early in your career, when these needs are simpler, begin to find those professionals who can serve as advisors and provide these professional services as needed, and with whom you can develop a trusting, personal, professional relationship.

The best source for these is often referrals. You can ask questions like, "Who do you know that can help with my taxes? I am looking to minimize taxes as well as file on time."

Or, "Who do you know that can provide legal advice for a contract I am reviewing for employment? For a new home purchase? For an apartment lease?" And so on.

Shape the referral questions to include specifics relating to your objectives in a particular field. "Who can you refer me with real estate expertise regarding leasing commercial property in the core city?" instead of "What Realtors do you know?" Ask more than one person for a referral. Interview more than one professional in each area to find the person who will listen to your objectives and provide the appropriate advice and service.

Another way to develop relationships with professionals is to serve on a committee or board of an organization outside of your business – a nonprofit organization serving the community, for example. These often attract professionals from different areas of expertise. You can observe them in action and possibly develop a personal, professional relationship before actually engaging them.

Early in your career, you will likely connect with a professional who is also relatively early in his or her own career. This is a great opportunity for the two of you to "grow" together.

When you find the right professional in an area, *hang on to them!* This will often require "intentionalizing" the relationship. Reach out for a meeting, breakfast, or coffee meet-up to update the professional even when immediate services are not needed. You will want to keep them informed of how things are developing so they are up to speed when services are needed.

Your relationship may only involve a few contacts a year, but understand that the relationship – and the professional's familiarity with your situation – can be critical when those services are suddenly, perhaps unexpectedly, needed on short notice.

The Details

During your career and your life, you will at various times need/benefit from calling on the specialized services of professionals in several key areas.

These areas may include:

- Financial (budgeting, choosing a financial institution, etc.)
- Investments
- Tax advice and filing
- Legal issues
- Real estate
- Insurance of all types (life, auto, property, personal liability, organizational liability, professional liability…). This may require separate insurance professionals for some specialized areas.
- Home or office tech management
- Career development

You will also most likely want to develop relationships with a:

- Medical doctor
- Dentist
- Ophthalmologist

As your career develops, look for opportunities to develop personal, professional relationships with individuals you trust in these and other areas where you may need specialty advice. This can and should be done before their services are needed on short notice or in critical situations.

Real-World Experience

<u>The purchase</u>

As my career took off, my income tax filing situation got more complex. Previously I was proud that I had done my own tax returns, but now due to complexity and time constraints, I decided to engage a tax professional. Through referrals I was introduced to Bob, a young accountant in a small firm. We developed rapport as my career advanced and Bob's practice grew. We served on the board of directors of two nonprofit organizations together.

Occasionally I felt I could do my tax returns myself and save the money, but I decided Bob's perspective, advice, and relationship were important, so I kept going to Bob. I kept him informed of my career development. I listened to his observations and advice about my career and personal finances.

At one point, I was given the opportunity to purchase the company I worked for. I quickly needed professional transaction advice. Bob now worked for a larger firm and quickly marshaled the resources for cash flow analysis and other transaction services. Bob helped me negotiate the purchase and later, when I sold the company, Bob referred me to professionals needed for that transaction.

The personal, professional relationship formed thirty years earlier, and maintained over that time, was critical to my business ownership, sale, and later management of investment funds derived from the company sale. It was also a satisfying relationship on a personal level.

The sale

I was invited to join the board of directors of a major nonprofit organization in my area. Despite difficult career time pressure, I agreed. While on the board, I met several professionals in different areas – including Robert, an attorney.

I engaged Robert to handle some relatively simple personal legal documents. I immediately liked his direct, straightforward style. When I purchased the company I was working for (see above Real-World Experience), I needed an ongoing corporate attorney for legal advice on contracts and other areas. I interviewed three attorneys, including Robert. I was again impressed by Robert's straightforward, professional manner, as well as his business legal experience. Our company engaged Robert as our corporate attorney.

Fortunately, the company seldom needed legal advice during the ten years that I owned it. However, I called on Robert whenever the need arose. Sometimes two years would go by without needing Robert's advice, but every year I invited Robert to dinner, jokingly stating this was his legal retainer for the year since our company hadn't officially used his services.

I used the conversation at dinner to update Robert on my personal and professional situation as well as update him on the company. I also expressed interest in how Robert's practice was developing. Where appropriate, I referred clients to him. We discussed other organizations we were currently involved in, as well as family updates.

When the opportunity to sell the company surfaced, I involved Robert in the transaction immediately. Thanks to my regular contact with him over the years, he knew many of the underlying issues associated with it. Our mutual trust – built over the years of our personal, professional relationship – facilitated communication. At a critical point in the sale, Robert gave me game-saving advice. This most likely would not have been possible if I had not had the ongoing relationship with Robert as a member of my personal board of advisors.

Resources

"Looking Out for Number One," article by Jim Collins, June 1996, www. jimcollins.com

Search "personal board of advisors" and you'll find many other information sources on this topic.

Get Started

1. Who do you consider members of your personal board of advisors?

2. What areas of expertise do you need to fill?

3. For the professionals you don't have in your network, who will you ask for referrals?

OKAY, I'VE READ ALL THIS STUFF... NOW WHAT?

The Overview

Congratulations! You've just given yourself a head start navigating in organizations; positively impacting organizations you choose to join; getting things done!

Get Started

Take out a sheet of paper (okay, I'm speaking metaphorically here. It doesn't have to be actual paper —it might be your laptop, tablet, smartphone…).

1. List things in this book that surprised you about navigating in organizations.

2. List things you think you are already doing effectively.

3. What do you need to improve on? What's holding you back from accomplishing your organizational objectives?

4. Looking back through the Get Started ideas and Resources indicated in this book, define specific actions you will take to be more effective.

Now do this:

1. List all the organizations you are currently part of or would like to be.

2. List your objectives <u>in</u> those organizations and <u>for</u> those organizations.

Take action!

Get organized!

Good luck!

ABOUT THE AUTHOR

Gary T. Moore began his organization career as Senior Patrol Leader of Boy Scout Troop 309. He began his working career as a co-operative engineering student at General Motors Institute (GMI...now Kettering University) at the age of seventeen, working in two General Motors assembly plants. He received a Bachelor of Electrical Engineering degree from GMI in 1969 and a Master of Science in Industrial Administration degree from Purdue University, Krannert School of Management, in 1970.

After five years of sales and marketing positions of increasing responsibility at the Allis Chalmers Corporation, he accepted the position of sales manager at Materials Handling Equipment Company, a locally owned industrial distributor in Denver, Colorado. After promotions to operations manager, executive vice president, general manager, and president, he purchased the company from its founders in 1997 and sold it to a larger distributor in 2006.

Gary has authored three books on sales and sales management in wholesale distribution and is a frequent author and speaker in the wholesale distribution industry.

Other leadership positions have included:

- **President, Board of Directors, Big Brothers of Metro Denver**

- **President, Board of Directors, Colorado I Have a Dream Foundation**

- **President, Board of Directors, Firefly Autism (aka Alta Vista Center for Autism Treatment)**

- **President, Board of Directors, Material Handling Equipment Distributors Association**

- **President, On Broadway Toastmasters**

- **Board member, Colorado Association of Commerce and Industry**

- **Board member, Denver Athletic Club**

- **Moderator, Sixth Avenue Community Church**

Gary and his wife Jane Costain live in Denver, Colorado.

His website is www.objectivebasedselling.net

He can be reached at garytrentm@aol.com

ACKNOWLEDGMENTS

Thanks to those who provided insight, input, and encouragement for this book:

Marilyn Anderson
Graphic designer

Deborah Dale Brackney
Executive Vice President,
Mountain States Employers Council

Jane Costain
My wife

David Dye www.trailblazeinc.com
Speaker, author, consultant

Bridget McCrea & Reba Hilbert
Editors

Kathryn "Katie" Richards
Student, Bradley University

Liz Richards
President,
Material Handling Equipment Distributors Association

Many of the staff of **Outskirts Press** www.outskirtspress.com

ACKNOWLEDGMENTS

Thanks to many who have provided positive examples and from whom I learned many of the principles in this book, including especially (in no particular order):

Ray Windas

Warner Frazier

Doug Vokes

Jack Patten

Robert Patten

Pres Askew

Jack Pink

Howard Bernstein

John Graham

Harry Neumann Jr

Ron Smith

Wayne Halligan

Ron Conrad

Wilma Moore (aka Mom)

Judy Russell Brown

Don Bray

Philip Puckett

Jesse Ogas

Don Bray

David Corsaut

Tim Tyler

Robert Hochstadt

Robert Loeb

Speedy

Tom Smith

Vicki Rains

Mary Hanewall

Charles C. Moore, Jr (aka Dad)

Those who have provided examples for the **Don't Section** of this book will go unnamed.

CPSIA information can be obtained
at www.ICGtesting.com
Printed in the USA
FSOW04n1522070316
17698FS